This book is dedicated to the following with
grateful thanks for all their enco~
and assistance

Dorothy Peters
Sidney Peters
Patricia Stamp
Mabel Lee

Contents

Introduction

The author was persuaded to write this book by the pleas for help from past Honorary Treasurers. They complained of the lack of simple information on book-keeping which would enable Treasurers to cope more adequately. Most have 'got by' through copying what was done in the previous year and, in the end, this practice is hardly likely to give the best results.

The reader will be expected to learn a few technical terms in the course of his reading, but otherwise no previous knowledge of book-keeping or accounting is assumed. To reinforce the learning process, there are a number of exercises for the reader to practise, applying his knowledge. Suggested solutions are provided so that each stage of his performance may be checked. All these techniques are brought together in a detailed example of the books and accounts of a typical club, in an Appendix at the end of the book. The schedules therein are referred to at intervals throughout the book.

The part played by the Honorary Auditor is also covered, as together they play a vital part in the successful running of any club.

In recent years charitable clubs and societies have become more popular, mainly for reasons of taxation, so that it was felt these justified a separate chapter.

Clubs incorporated under the Companies Acts 1948 to 1980 or registered under the Friendly Societies Act 1974, or the Industrial & Provident Societies Acts 1965 to 1978, are not covered by this book.

All names and societies, associations, clubs, organisations or individuals mentioned in this book are entirely fictional and in no way represent any living persons or existing organisations.

CHAPTER 1

The End Product

It may be thought somewhat strange to start a book by talking about the end product, by which is meant the final information that is produced by an accounting system – what the Accountant calls the **final accounts**. Perhaps it is not quite so strange when it is realised that the accounting system must be tailored to meet these requirements. However, before we can discuss and design any system, we need to know exactly what types of final accounts these are, and what purposes they serve.

Let us assume that the society or association is a fairly typical one with members' subscriptions and the proceeds from socials as the main sources of income, while the payments are standard to the extent that they are common to most organisations. A good name might be 'The Bee Sting Society' with some forty-five members who meet at the local social club once a month.

The information needs of such a society will be relatively simple. Most members will be concerned with keeping the subscriptions at a modest level and making sure that there is a reasonable amount of money in hand and at the Bank at the end of the year. When the annual accounts are presented at the annual general meeting, a summary form of accounts will probably be sufficient. Should any of the members ask for details of any particular item, the Hon. Treasurer can usually oblige with an explanation which will be suitable.

To meet this type of need, a summary of the 'Receipts and Payments for the Year' is sufficient. A **Receipts and Payments account** is merely the totals of the Cash and Bank receipts and payments being combined to give total figures. The amount of analysis required is fairly small as there will be relatively few types of expenditure. Perhaps the simple example on page 3 will help.

The main problem with the account shown in Fig. 1 is that it does not show whether there are any outstanding bills or income at the end of the year. Of course, a simple way to show such information would be to put a note at the foot of the account saying something like 'There are outstanding bills to be paid of £X for ——'. Alternatively, the note might read 'Unpaid subscriptions relating to the year of £7 are still outstanding'.

If the club or society owns any assets, these too are not shown by a Receipts and Payments account. Many organisations own various types of equipment and some own property worth a good deal of money. In these circumstances it is misleading not to show the full position of the organisation. Not only is it important to see whether an

Fig. 1

BEE STING SOCIETY

Receipts and Payments Account for the Year ended 31 December 19 . .

	£			£	£
Monies in Hand 1 January			Hon. Secretary's expenses		7
Cash	£17		Postages & stationery		13
At Bank	57	74	Hire of room		24
Members' subscriptions			Loss on magazine sales		23
(44 @ £1.50)		66			
Annual dance (Net)		36	Subscription to Bees Knees		
Whist drives		39	Association		5
			Coach trip		27
			Monies in Hand 31 December		
			Cash	12	
			At Bank	104	116
		£215			£215

organisation is making or losing money, but its assets and liabilities need to be known in order for the organisation to be properly managed. Sometimes the two aspects of the same thing are like looking at a stick of seaside rock. The lurid-coloured stick has a length which represents the accounting year. We can give a precise figure for its length, just as we can give a precise figure for the overall performance of a society or association for the year. If the seaside rock is then turned so that we can read the words shown in the rock at its sectional view, this represents the asset/liability position. Thus, there are two entirely different ways of looking at exactly the same thing.

To enable these two aspects of an organisation to be shown in terms of annual accounts, the Accountant prepares two accounts which are linked together to form a 'whole'. These are an **Income and Expenditure account** and **Balance Sheet**. The former is able to make adjustments for those outstanding expenses or income, while the Balance Sheet shows the assets and liabilities.

For anyone with a degree of familiarity with commercial accounts, the Income and Expenditure is similar in principle to the commercial 'Profit and Loss account'. Instead of measuring the net profit or loss for a trading year, the Income and Expenditure account measures the excess of income over expenditure or the excess of expenditure over income for the year.

To appreciate the difference between the relatively simple Receipts and Payments account, let us see how this can be turned into an Income and Expenditure account, with a few minor additional items (see Fig. 2). We will assume that at 31 December there was a further £9 hire of the room due, and the Social Secretary says that she still has £5 to go into the Bank from past whist drives.

There are several obvious points about the difference between these accounts and those shown in Fig. 1. The receipts and payments seem to have changed sides and may look wrong. The reason is that the Accountant has *completed the double entry*. This is a system of recording accounting transactions twice, as it recognises that each transaction

Fig. 2

BEE STING SOCIETY

Income and Expenditure Account for the Year ended 31 December 19..

	£			£
Hon. Secretary's expenses	7	Members subscriptions		
Postage & stationery	13	(44 @ £1.50)		66
Hire of room (24 + 9)	33	Annual dance (Net)		36
Loss on sale of magazines	23	Whist drives (39 + 5)		44
Subscription to Bees Knees Association	5			
Coach trip	27			
	108			
Excess of Income over Expenditure				
for the year	38			
	£146			£146

Balance Sheet as at 31 December 19..

Accumulated Fund	£	*Current Assets*	£	£
Balance 1 January	74	Monies in Hand		
Add Excess of Income over		Cash	12	
Expenditure for the year	38	At Bank	104	116
	112	Debtor re whist drive		5
Current Liabilities				
Creditor for hire of room	9			
	£121			£121

can be viewed from two points of view. More will be said later on about this system, but it is sufficient to say that full accounts kept on that basis have great advantages as they can deal with all accounting problems and give accurate information.

The Accumulated Fund represents the net investment of members of the organisation. In the case of a limited company it would be the amount of share capital and accumulated reserves held by the shareholders. In the simple example above, it has been assumed that the society did not own any assets such as equipment, so that the Accumulated Fund merely reflects the main assets of cash in hand and at the Bank. Had the Society additional assets, then they would have been reflected there as well as in the existing assets.

A source of amazement to many people is that both sides of a Balance Sheet balance. It is really quite simple when it is realised that 'double entry' means entering the same amount twice, so that like an equation it must balance.

One important point about a Balance Sheet is that it is not a ledger account or even an account, it is strictly a classified list of the balances remaining in the books after the prior accounts, like the Income and Expenditure, have been closed off.

By now the reader should be able to appreciate that there are two major types of information available to him, the Receipts and Payments account on its own, and the

Income and Expenditure account with related Balance Sheet. It is for him and members of the organisation to decide which is the right type for their particular needs, bearing in mind that it is the Hon. Treasurer who actually has to do the work. His views might be worth considering.

From this point on the main method of book-keeping will be shown, with detailed examples to enable a Treasurer to prepare either a Receipt and Payments account with no further knowledge of book-keeping or, if he is more ambitious, to go all the way to the Income and Expenditure account with Balance Sheet. The choice is his.

CHAPTER 2

Background to Book-keeping

Book-keeping may be defined as the recording in the books of account of a business or organisation the day-to-day financial transactions as they take place. The extent of the book-keeping will depend on the type of organisation and its 'information needs'. This means the type and extent of the information that is required from its fundamental records. In the case of a limited company, this is largely laid down in the Companies Act 1948 Schedule 8, as amended. The 'information needs' of clubs and social organisations will range from a simple Bank summary at the end of the year up to a detailed Income and Expenditure account with Balance Sheet and supporting schedules.

The boundary between accounting and book-keeping is clearly defined by the **trial balance**. Once the book-keeper has finished making the entries in his books of account, he will 'balance' each ledger account and insert this figure in the trial balance. If both sides of the trial balance agree, or add up to the same total, it is prima facie confirmation that he has done his work correctly.

It is the task of the Accountant to take the trial balance submitted to him by the book-keeper and then to go through the ledgers closing off the accounts as he prepares the final accounts in whatever form these take.

Having looked at the nature of book-keeping, something must be said about the underlying principles. The most fundamental of these is **double entry**. This was devised over four hundred years ago to deal with the situation whereby every financial transaction may be regarded from two points of view. Every transaction is therefore a combination of two of the following:

1 Asset
2 Liability
3 Loss or expense
4 Profit or gain

Take a simple example of purchasing a packet of cigarettes. You incur the liability to pay in cash, yet at the same time you acquire an asset of equal value although it is the same transaction.

Another case would be the payment of your telephone bill. This time you still have a liability to pay in cash, but instead of purchasing an asset of equal value you have incurred an expense of equal value.

Double entry will be clearly illustrated later in this chapter together with the appropriate rules. Meanwhile it is sufficient to say that as a system of book-keeping it has proved to be a very valuable and reliable method over the centuries. One of the great merits is that the book-keeper is able to prove the accuracy of his work by means of the trial balance already mentioned.

The second of the important principles of book-keeping concerns the point of view from which the book-keeping is undertaken. Here it is vital to appreciate that the members of an organisation are separate from the organisation itself. The book-keeping is from the point of view of the organisation, looking outwards towards the members. Failure to appreciate this basic but simple fact will mean that the reader will either fail to properly understand book-keeping, or will literally do it backwards. The author has seen the results of such a system in practice, and while it will work if everything is reversed, the result to the average person could be described as 'confusing'.

The means of recording information in books of account is the **ledger account** which is sometimes known as the **'T' account**. This is because of the ruling lines shown below:

Debit (Dr.)   Credit (Cr.)

A ledger account is a sheet of paper with a line down the middle and provision made at the top for entering the title of the account, for example, a Cash account:

Cash Account
Dr.   Cr.

The word 'account' is normally omitted as this is understood by users.

The two sides of the ledger account are known as **debit** and **credit** respectively, with the contractions **Dr.** and **Cr.** for convenience. These terms must be learned as they will be used throughout this book.

A ledger account is a type of 'file' for financial information, and just as you will have a separate file for each separate matter, a new ledger account will be opened whenever a different type of transaction is undertaken. All transactions of a similar nature will appear on the same ledger sheet. Thus, all receipts and payments by cheque will appear on the one Bank account, but there will be as many separate ledger accounts as are needed to correctly analyse this information.

What then are the rules to enable entries to be made correctly? Surprisingly there are four basic rules, and while they may appear to be simple their initial application by the reader may give rise to much frustration. With this in mind, it is recommended that the reader should copy out the rules and put them within easy reach so that they can be referred to frequently.

The rules are as follows:

1 Debit assets
2 Debit losses and expenses
3 Credit liabilities
4 Credit profits and gains

A short example may help. Members of the E.F.G. Tennis Club contributed £450 cash to the Club to purchase equipment valued at £300, £60 for rent and £30 for tennis-balls. The sum of £55 is received in subscriptions.

First, a Cash account will be needed, and also a form of **'Capital' account** so two 'T' accounts should be drawn up:

Cash				Capital			
	£						£
Capital	450					Cash	450

These entries record the borrowing of £450 from the Club Members and the receipt of the cash itself. What decides the side of an account on which an entry is to be made? First, consider the nature of both ends of the transaction: the asset cash was received. Rule 1 says that assets are debited so that entry will appear on the debit side of the Cash account. At the same time the £450 has been borrowed from the Members so that the Club has incurred a liability to repay that money if the Club should be wound up in the future. Hence the 'Capital' account is credited in accordance with rule 3.

The word 'Capital' has been shown in inverted commas as it is more usual to describe that account in a social organisation as the **Accumulated Fund**, but this term may sound misleading if used in the context of a brand new organisation. In any business context it would be correct to use the term 'Capital', and in the case of a limited company it would be the Share Capital account.

To record the purchase of the equipment will require an **Equipment account** to be opened as this is a different type of transaction, although the cash payment aspect can be made on the Cash account.

The cumulative position is thus:

Cash					Capital			
	£			£				£
Capital	450	Equipment		300			Cash	450
Equipment								
	£							
Cash	300							

It will be noticed that alongside each entry there is a word describing the account on which the opposite entry will be found. This would also normally have some reference number, like a page number, to enable cross-reference to be made.

The reasoning behind the latest entry is that the Equipment account is debited in accordance with rule 1, as equipment is the nature of the item purchased, and it is important to analyse our receipts and payments. The credit entry on the Cash account reflects the liability, in accordance with rule 3, to discharge the debt in cash.

The payments for rent and the purchase of tennis-balls are both expenses. This means that the 'benefit' of such expenditure is of fairly short duration; in the case of the rent, perhaps for a month or three months, while the tennis-balls will have a limited life. This is in contrast to the much longer period of use that one might expect from the more expensive equipment which one regards as an asset. This is a fundamental distinction which the reader must be prepared to make as the accounting treatment is so completely different. The expense item will go in the Income and Expenditure account while the asset will appear in the Balance Sheet.

The accounts are now beginning to build up, so that the latest position cumulatively is as follows:

Cash

	£		£
Capital	450	Equipment	300
		Rent	60
		Tennis-balls	30

Capital

			£
		Cash	450

Equipment

	£		
Cash	300		

Rent

	£		
Cash	60		

Tennis-balls

	£		
Cash	30		

These expense payments follow rule 2 in that being expenses they are debited. In each case there is the liability to pay in cash, hence they are credited to the Cash account.

The final entry in this short example is the £55 received by the Club in respect of Members' subscriptions. The cash received, being an asset, is debited to the Cash account as per rule 1, while the credit entry will be made in the Subscriptions account as per rule 4, being a profit or gain.

The cash-book position thus looks like this:

Cash

	£		£
Capital	450	Equipment	300
Subscriptions	55	Rent	60
		Tennis-balls	30

The credit entry to the Subscriptions is as under

Subscriptions

		£
	Cash	55

At this stage there are two further lessons to be learned:

(1) How to balance a ledger account
(2) How to prepare the trial balance

We start with the Cash account which should look like this:

Cash

	£		£
Capital	450	Equipment	300
Subscriptions	55	Rent	60
		Tennis-balls	30
			390
		Balance carried down	115
	£505		£505
Balance brought down	115		

This procedure is called **balancing the account**. The purpose is to find out the net amount between the two sides, and in the case of a Cash account it must be brought down as a debit balance as one cannot spend more cash than one possesses, in contrast to a Bank overdraft which would be brought down as a credit balance.

The procedure is to put a single line beneath the payments to make a subtotal (£390 in the illustration). Then the words 'Balance carried down' are inserted, and a gap left for the insertion of the balance figure. Single lines followed by a gap, and then double lines all on the same level should be drawn up. The purpose of the double lines is to indicate that one has ceased to use all the figures above them.

The receipts side is totalled (£505) and the same figure inserted at the foot of the opposite column. The total payments (£390) are deducted, and the balance (£115) is then inserted in the vacant space. Note that the balance is then brought down below the double lines, taking care that the balance figure is in alignment with the rest of that column of figures. Failure to do this will result in difficulties with the addition of the receipts side in the following period, as the figures will be out of alignment.

Where a ledger account has figures on one side only, for the purpose of the trial balance there is no balancing action required, merely a subtotal of these figures.

The trial balance can now be prepared for the above ledger accounts:

Trial Balance	Dr. £	Cr. £
Cash	115	
Capital		450
Equipment	300	
Rent	60	
Tennis-balls	30	
Subscriptions		55
	£505	£505

With the agreement of the two totals the book-keeper can relax as he is able to say that, on the face of things, he appears to have done his work correctly. Unfortunately, there are four types of book-keeping errors which do not affect the totals of the trial balance, but which may materially affect the accuracy of the accounts. These errors are:

(a) Errors of omission
(b) Errors of principle
(c) Compensating errors
(d) Errors of commission

Hence, a cautious note of self-congratulation if the trial balance does agree.

It is important to know exactly what a trial balance is and what are its limitations. It is simply a memoranda list of the balances in the ledger accounts after the book-keeper has finished making the day-to-day entries. The trial balance is not in any way a ledger account. It is normally prepared at regular and convenient intervals such as the end of the month or the end of the year. Apart from acting as an arithmetical check on the accuracy of the book-keeping, the trial balance also serves the purpose of acting as a basis for the Accountant, enabling him to close off the various ledger accounts and prepare the final accounts.

The book-keeping errors mentioned above need a little explanation as they may pass unnoticed, and yet have a material effect on the accuracy of the accounts.

An *error of omission* is where a transaction has been omitted completely from the accounting system. Thus, a sales invoice may be made out for a customer and yet never get into the sales day-book or the sales ledger because it has been mislaid or inadvertently destroyed.

Errors of principle are particularly serious as they materially affect the distinction between the Income and Expenditure account and the Balance Sheet. If the former is debited with substantial expenditure for alleged repairs, but which should be treated as improvements and additions to property, the effect is that the Income and Expenditure will have been wrongly charged with the expense, and the Balance Sheet will not show the true value of the property. In the commercial world this may affect the tax position and, in the case of a public company, where a sum is material, it may even affect a Stock Exchange quotation or the price of shares on the Stock Exchange.

Compensating errors are disconcerting as if one is discovered, by definition, there must be others around. Errors of this category cancel themselves out. Thus, both sides of a trial balance may be under or over added by £100. If you discover the debit error, the credit error may be the combination of one or more errors.

Errors of commission are less serious, but none the less are errors. These are errors within the same type of ledger account. In commercial firms the wrong customer may be debited with a sales invoice; the Balance Sheet still shows correctly the total debts due to the business, but one customer rejoices because he has not received a bill, whilst another may be very irate at being sent a bill for goods he did not order or receive.

The reader is invited to work through the following exercises and compare the results with the suggested solutions.

Exercise

THE PAT BALL TENNIS CLUB

The following are the cash transactions during the months of June to August of the Club, whose first season started on 1 June.

			£
June	1	Received Members' subscriptions	84
	5	First instalment of rent paid for hire of courts	25
	10	Purchase of tennis-balls	34
	22	Received further Members' subscriptions	75
	25	Purchase of refreshments for resale	23
July	3	Received donation towards Club expenses	100
	5	Purchase of tennis-balls	22
	10	Paid Secretary's expenses	17
	10	Paid second instalment of Club rent	25
	10	Purchase of stationery	12
	22	Received proceeds of sale of refreshments	8
	31	Purchased sundries, including a post and net	7
Aug.	1	Received new Members' subscriptions	26
	3	Purchase of refreshments for resale	9
	12	Expenditure on Club dance	41
	17	Sale of dance tickets	57
	25	Received proceeds of sale of refreshments	27
	31	Paid final instalment of rent	42

You are required to write up the Cash account completing the double entry in the appropriate ledger accounts, and to prepare a trial balance.

THE PAT BALL TENNIS CLUB

Suggested solution

(*a*)

Cash Account

		£				£
June 1	Subscriptions	84	June 5	Rent 1st instalment	25
22	Subscriptions	75	10	Purchase of tennis-balls	34
July 3	Donation received	100	25	Purchase of refreshments	23
22	Proceeds sale of refreshments	8	July 5	Purchase of tennis-balls	22
			10	Secretary's expenses	17
Aug. 1	Subscriptions	26	10	Rent 2nd instalment	25
17	Proceeds sale of dance tickets	57	10	Purchase of stationery	12
			31	Sundries, including post and net	7
25	Proceeds sale of refreshments	27	Aug. 3	Purchase of refreshments	9
			12	Expenditure re Club dance	41
			31	Rent – final instalment	42
					257
				Balance c/d	120
		£377			**£377**
Balance b/d		120			

Subscriptions			
			£
June 1	Cash		84
22	do.		75
Aug. 1	do.		26
			185

Rent			
			£
June 5	Cash		25
July 10	do.		25
Aug. 31	do.		42
			92

Tennis-balls			
			£
June 10	Cash		34
July 5	do.		22
			56

Refreshments						
		£				£
June 25	Cash	23	July 22	Cash		8
Aug. 3	do.	9	Aug. 25	do.		27
Balance c/d		3				
		£35				**£35**
			Balance b/d			3

Dance						
		£				£
Aug. 12	Cash	41	Aug. 17	Cash		57
Balance c/d		16				
		£57				**£57**
			Balance b/d			16

Donation received		
		£
July 3 Cash		100

Secretary's expenses		
		£
July 10 Cash		17

Stationery		
		£
July 10 Cash		12

Sundries		
		£
July 31 Cash		7

(*b*)

Trial Balance

	Dr. £	Cr. £
Cash account	120	
Subscriptions		185
Rent	92	
Tennis-balls	56	
Refreshments		3
Dance		16
Donation received		100
Secretary's expenses	17	
Stationery	12	
Sundries	7	
	£304	£304

Exercise

THE POSTAGE STAMP CLUB

The following were the cash transactions of the Club during the Autumn session from 1 October to 31 December.

			£
Oct.	1	Balance in hand	49
	2	Printing Autumn programme	14
	3	Purchase of refreshments	13
	3	Rent	10
	7	Received Members' subscriptions	29
	15	Receipts from special lecture	15
	15	Lecturer's expenses	9
	25	Repairs to overhead projector	16
	31	Sale of refreshments	5
Nov.	3	Rent	10
	8	Received Members' subscriptions	35
	14	Secretary's expenses	18
	17	Proceeds from film show	9
	25	Purchase of refreshments	4
Dec.	3	Rent	10
	5	Purchase of notice board	27
	9	Proceeds of raffle	16
	14	ditto	3
	14	Stationery	11
	17	Sale of refreshments	5
	23	Donation received	10
	29	Sale of refreshments	3

You are required to write up the Cash account, completing the double entry in the appropriate ledger accounts, and to prepare a trial balance.

THE POSTAGE STAMP CLUB

Suggested solution

(a)

Cash account

			£				£
Oct.	1	Balance b/f	49	Oct.	2	Printing of Autumn	
	7	Members' subscriptions	29			programme	14
	15	Receipts from special			3	Rent	10
		lecture	15		3	Purchase of refreshments	13
	31	Proceeds of sale of			15	Lecturer's expenses	9
		refreshments	5		25	Repairs to overhead	
Nov.	8	Members' subscriptions	35			projector	16
	17	Proceeds of film show	9	Nov.	3	Rent	10
Dec.	9	Proceeds of raffle	16		14	Secretary's expenses	18
	14	ditto	3		25	Purchase of refreshments	4
	17	Proceeds of sale of		Dec.	3	Rent	10
		refreshments	5		5	Purchase of notice-board	27
	23	Donation received	10		14	Stationery	11
	29	Proceeds of sale of					142
		refreshments	3		31	Balance c/d	37
			£179				£179
Dec.	31	Balance b/d	37				

Printing and stationery

			£
Oct.	2	Cash	14
Dec.	14	do.	11
			25

Refreshments

			£				£
Oct.	13	Cash	13	Oct.	31	Cash	5
Nov.	25	do.	4	Dec.	17	do.	5
					29	do.	3
						Balance c/d	4
			£17				£17
Balance b/d			4				

Rent

			£
Oct.	3	Cash	10
Nov.	3	do.	10
Dec.	3	do.	10
			30

Repairs to equipment

			£
Oct.	25	Cash	16

Donation received

			£
	Dec. 23	Cash	10

Members' subscriptions

			£
Oct.	7	Cash	29
Nov.	8	do.	35
			64

Sundry receipts

		£				£
Oct. 15	Cash	9	Oct.	15	Cash	15
Balance c/d		15	Nov.	17	do.	9
		£24				£24
			Balance b/d			15

Raffle

			£
	Dec.	9	Cash	16
		14	do.	3
			19

Secretary's expenses

		£
Nov. 14	Cash	18

New equipment

		£
Dec. 5	Cash	27

Accumulated fund

		£
Oct. 1	Balance b/f	49

(b

Trial Balance	Dr. £	Cr. £
Cash account	37	
Printing and stationery	25	
Members' subscriptions		64
Refreshments	4	
Sundry receipts		15
Raffle		19
Rent	30	
Secretary's expenses	18	
Repairs to equipment	16	
Donation received		10
New equipment	27	
Accumulated Fund		49
	£157	£157

Note

Since the Cash account had a balance brought forward (£49) on 1 October, it is assumed that the corresponding credit balance was represented by the Accumulated Fund or Capital account. Contrast this with the Cash account in the Pat Ball Tennis Club example where there was no prior balance.

CHAPTER 3

The Basic Books

The Analysed Cash-book

In Chapter 2 the preparation of a Cash account was explained. This involved two stages. First, the Cash account had to be written up and balanced, and then the double entry had to be completed in respect of each receipt and payment. The completion of this double entry meant opening a new ledger account each time a new category of information was involved. Thus cash receipts for capital and sales required separate accounts to record the different natures of the two receipts, although the asset itself, the cash, was recorded in both cases in the Cash account. This was because it was physical cash received each time.

Cash accounts are important, and later this will be the subject of a separate section (see page 23), but the majority of financial transactions are carried out by means of cheques. These have many advantages, as they enable large sums of money to be paid without the risk of theft, and also they avoid the problems of carrying bulky or heavy loads of cash. Consequently it is now necessary to consider the use of a **Bank account**.

In layout the Bank account is identical to the Cash account. Later, one major difference will appear in connection with balancing the Bank account. If there is an overdraft at the end of a period, this will show as a credit balance brought down, which of course is impossible with a Cash account. This is because it is physically impossible to spend more cash than you have in hand, but quite possible to draw out more money than you have standing to your credit in the Bank provided the Bank has agreed to your overdraft facilities.

It is not proposed to give any examples of a Bank account, as reference to the Cash account of the 'Postage Stamp Club' illustrated at the end of Chapter 2 would easily double as a Bank account.

For the purpose of this book, what is important to realise is that when a Bank account is laid out in the manner of those Cash accounts which have been illustrated, it necessitates the double entry being completed in a suitable ledger account for every receipt and payment. Where transactions are routine and repetitive this leads to a lot of entries being made, which can be avoided by using suitably designed Bank accounts.

At this stage it is necessary to learn further accounting terminology. Reference will be made in this book to the **cash-book**. This term is widely used in book-keeping and accounting circles, but is somewhat misleading. It may refer to a book containing either Bank *and* cash transactions or merely Bank transactions *alone*. Cash transactions tend to be small in number and in amount, and will be recorded in the **petty-cash book**, hence its title.

If the cash-book is designed properly, much of the double-entry detail can be accumulated in the cash-book itself so that at the end of a period the book is added up and the totals under each heading are debited or credited in place of the numerous details under the previous system. A cash-book designed in this manner is known as an **analysis cash-book** and has a number of additional columns to provide the analysis. The procedure is to enter the date of the transaction in the date column, and either the name of the payee or the nature of the transaction in the details column. The total amount is then entered twice, once in the total column and again under the appropriate analysis column. Reference should be made to the Frendlee Club example, Schedule (I) in the Appendix, where it will be clearly seen how this is done. To ensure that the reader fully understands this, two extracts will suffice.

On 25 October the payment to Records Ltd of £25.75 appears under the total column and the analysis column headed 'Records'.

The receipts side illustrates a particularly useful feature. Note how the sale of refreshments and receipts from billiards and table tennis recur at very frequent intervals. Take the total of £7.58 on 21 February, analysed under these heads. This analysis saves separate entries to three separate ledgers each time money is banked. Instead, the total at the end of the year will be entered in the ledger accounts so that £113.50 would go to the credit of billiards receipts and £44.85 to table tennis receipts. (See Frendlee Club example, Schedule (H) in the Appendix.)

The purpose of these multi-column analysis books is therefore to save a considerable amount of clerical labour. In book-keeping terms, the total column in each case represents the ledger account, while the analysis columns are strictly memoranda, the double entry being completed when the totals of these columns are entered in the ledger accounts.

At this stage the reader is invited to 'tick' (see page 27 for explanation of this term) through the totals in the cash-book of the Frendlee Club into the ledger accounts. In this way he will discover for himself the general procedure.

Something needs to be said about the various rulings and types of cash-books available.

Generally speaking, any cash-book will have a minimum need of a date column, detail column, reference or voucher number column and a total column. The number of analysis columns required will depend on the nature of a Club's requirements. There should be sufficient columns to allow for additional future analysis needs.

To allow for items which will not fit under any other convenient heading, both sides of the cash-book should include an analysis column marked 'N.L.' or 'nominal ledger'. This column is not a 'sundries' or 'dustbin' account, but rather it is a column into which are put either items of special importance or those which may need to be dealt with by the Accountant separately at the end of the year. Meanwhile, it enables the book-keeper to complete his cash-book entries without further worry.

Club Treasurers sometimes ask whether the receipts and payments in the cash-book should be in different parts of the book, or whether they should have a ruling that will show both, side by side. There is no clear-cut answer to the question as a great deal will depend on the individual information needs of each club. As a general rule, it can be said that the receipts and payments appearing in different parts of the analysis cash-book have the advantage that more analysis columns can be provided for each side.

These days, analysis cash-books come in different types. The Treasurer has the choice of a fairly slim volume of some hundred pages or, alternatively, a loose-leaf volume. The former is perhaps helpful where the volume of transactions annually is fairly small, as it is light and easy to carry. The loose-leaf variety have a great advantage in that old sheets can be taken out and new sheets inserted if a particular section has more entries than another. Some clubs may have more receipts being entered than payments. Hence, more pages can be inserted in the receipts section if required.

The Treasurer should consult his stationer about the types of cash-books available and discuss the printed rulings which would be most suited to his needs. There is a wide variety of both.

The task of preparing a Bank reconciliation to prove the accuracy of the writing up of the cash-book is an important one which must be done at regular intervals. The chapter on this topic should now be read carefully.

The Imprest System of Petty Cash *

This is a system of cash control which is widely used to ensure that the person handling it has a limited responsibility. Such a person is known in business and commercial organisations as the **Petty Cashier**, as the sums involved are relatively small.

The basic principle is that the Petty Cashier is given a fixed **float**. This is a sum of money for which he is responsible, and he must be able to account for the money spent and the remaining cash. The amount spent is reimbursed exactly at convenient intervals by means of a separate cheque drawn for cash so that the 'float' is restored to its original size.

This method protects an organisation from loss on an unlimited scale, and likewise limits the responsibility of the Petty Cashier so that the risk or temptation of fraud is reduced.

The first question in setting up such a system is to decide the amount of the float. In a large organisation this may be £1000 or more, while in the case of a small club £5 may be sufficient. The sum should be large enough to deal with day-to-day cash

Petty-Cash

Date	Details	Total	Date	Detail	Voucher No.	Total
		£				£
Dec. 1	Balance b/f	150.00	Dec. 1	Jim Brown	273	5.75
				Sue Smith	274	6.41
			3	Stamps	275	10.20
			5	Ron Chambers	276	4.26
31	Bank CB151	132.61		Supermarket Ltd	277	8.19
			9	Future Products Co. – balloons	278	3.75
			10	Smith & Co. – beer mats	279	2.17
			11	Jean Fish	280	3.47
				Window Cleaning Co.	281	8.00
			14	Jim Brain	282	4.30
				Sheila Johnson	283	5.20
			17	Future Products Co. – party novelties	284	9.16
			18	Future Products Co. – balloons for Xmas decorations	285	14.61
				Elsie Waters	286	4.65
			21	Harper & Co. – prizes	287	12.24
				Edwards & Co. – cocktail sticks	288	1.39
			22	Jean Fish	289	4.74
				Stationer's Ltd – menu forms & receipt book	290	3.80
			24	Lewis Mann	291	7.80
				Supermarket Ltd	292	6.52
			31	Stamps	293	6.00
						132.61
				Balance c/d		150.00
		£282.61				£282.61
Dec. 31	Balance b/d	150.00				

WORKING MEN'S CLUB

Book

Casual Wages	Cleaning Expenses	Postage & Stationery	Social & Party Expenses	Re Xmas Festivities	Bar Items	N.L.
£	£	£	£	£	£	£
5.75						
6.41						
		10.20				
4.26						
	8.19					
			3.75			
					2.17	
3.47						
	8.00					
4.30						
5.20						
				9.16		
			3.75	10.86		
4.65				12.24		
					1.39	
4.74						
		3.80				
7.80						
	6.52					
		6.00				
£46.58	£22.71	£20.00	£7.50	£32.26	£3.56	

payments, allowing a reasonable length of time between each reimbursement. This may be weekly in a busy organisation, or every two or three months in the case of a club.

The equipment required will be a ruled petty-cash book somewhat similar in appearance to the analysis cash-book. The usual difference will be that only one or two debit columns will be required and with a limited number of credit colums. Once again there is a wide choice of rulings available, and your stationer will be pleased to advise you on your requirements.

In addition to the petty-cash book, proper petty-cash vouchers should also be used. These can be purchased in small blocks or packs and are usually coloured for convenience. As each payment is made, the Petty Cashier should fill in a voucher with the details of the payment, the date and the name of the person receiving the money. That person should then sign the voucher which will be given a number before being filed away. The number will be the sequence number of the payment as the details are entered in the petty-cash book.

In addition to the signature of the person receiving the payment, any documentary evidence of the transaction should be attached to the voucher. Thus, any bills, invoices, statements or till-roll receipts should be stapled to the voucher.

As part of the system of control, many organisations rule that if expenditure beyond a fixed amount is incurred, the countersignature of a senior official or other person will be required. The advantage of such a rule is that the Petty Cashier is protected from criticism if later the transaction is questioned or challenged.

While on the subject of control, it is important to arrange an additional check of the Petty Cashier's float. This should be an inspection carried out at regular intervals by a senior official. Of prime importance is that the inspection should take place in the presence of the Petty Cashier, as if there is a 'difference' or an unaccountable loss of cash it is very easy for accusations to be made.

Should there be more than one petty-cash box in use in an organisation, then these should be examined at the same time. The author recalls the problem of trying to count the floats held by eight members of staff of a large hotel where some staff came in early in the morning and others late at night. Fraud was suspected, but the time difference made it almost impossible to establish.

The Take-it-Easy Working Mens' Club example on pages 20 and 21 illustrates a typical layout of a petty-cash account.

There are several points to notice. First, the cheque received of £132.61 to reimburse the expenditure should be drawn specifically for this purpose. No transfer should be made from cash takings as all takings should be banked in full.

The second point is that at convenient intervals the payments analysis can be ruled off and the totals transferred to the debit of the respective ledger expense accounts. Alternatively, the totals are left running, page by page, and in these circumstances no balance will be carried down. Instead, after reimbursement, the difference between the debit and credit columns will merely be equal to the amount of the float.

The Cash Account

The analysed cash-book and the imprest system of petty cash described so far are designed to deal with an efficient handling of club finance. The basic principles are that all receipts, whether of cash or cheques, are banked intact and that all sums paid out exceeding a fairly nominal amount are paid by cheque. The Frendlee Club illustration is based on these assumptions. However, it is realised that there will be situations beyond the control of the Treasurer who is obliged to handle larger sums of cash, both receipts and payments. He requires the means of coping with these situations, and the answer does not lie with an imprest system of petty cash.

What is required is an analysed Cash account, much on the lines of the analysed Bank account so that, if necessary, the two can be linked together. The Cash account of The Social Club on pages 24 and 25 is a short example with most of the features required.

Starting with the balance brought forward of £57.50 on 1 January, it will be noted that this is extended into the nominal ledger column. This is merely to ensure that when each column is down cast, the totals will cross cast to the total of the total column. (Remember that the nominal ledger account provides a column for large exceptional items or items for which there is no other suitable column.)

The illustration shows two methods of recording subscriptions. In extending the figures to the Subscriptions analysis column (Subs.), one might use the total as in the case of the £45 on 3 January, or individually as on 10 January.

Of particular importance to some Treasurers is the entry on 4 January showing a net receipt from David Parker of £60.70. Deductions from receipts before they are received are difficult to record without the use of a journal, an accounting book which has only limited uses in the commercial accounting world. Probably the best method for the Club Treasurer is to record the facts in the Detail column, and extend into the appropriate receipts column the gross receipt. At the same time the payment already deducted must be recorded as a payment on the payments side of the cash-book. Thus, in the example the receipt in the Dances column is shown at the full £70 and the dance expenses of £9.30 as a payment under 'Expenses re Dances'.

Both sides of the cash-book have a column marked 'Bank Contra'. These are to enable the Bank account and the Cash account to be linked. The £100 paid into the Bank on 17 January would be debited in the Bank account. Should the Treasurer require cash from the Bank, he would draw a cash cheque entered on the credit side of the Bank and debited on the Cash account.

In the illustration no 'balance' has been brought down to find the difference between the two sides. This can be easily worked out on a scrap of paper. Not bringing down a balance until the Balance Sheet date or any other convenient date enables the totals to be carried forward without interruption page after page, giving useful information on receipts and payments to date. When the columns are finally ruled off, the totals of the analysis columns will need to be posted to the ledger. The items in the nominal ledger columns will be posted individually.

(a) Receipts

THE SOCIAL CLUB
Cash Account

Year 1		Detail	Total	Bank Contra	Subs.	Sun-dries	Proceeds of Raffles	Dances	Socials	Dona-tions	Sale of Refresh-ments	N.L.
		£	£	£	£	£	£	£	£	£	£	£
Jan. 1	Balance – Cash in Hand		57.50									57.50
3	George Smith	4.50										
	Amanda Mason	4.50										
	Hilary Jones	4.50										
	Jean Lowe	4.50										
	Pat Jones	4.50										
	Derrick Johnson	4.50										
	Stan Jones	4.50										
	Peter Lowe	4.50										
	Jean Corns	4.50										
	Hilary James	4.50	45.00		45.00							
4	David Parker – sale of dance tickets 35 @ £2.00	70.00										
	Less expenses	9.30										
		60.70	70.00					70.00				
7	Mrs Fry – donation in memory of her late husband		50.00							50.00		
10	John Sinclair	4.50										
	Sheila Deane	4.50										
	Janet Watson	4.50										
	Lisa Williams	4.50										
	Tea Committee – sale of refreshments	6.41	24.41								6.41	
14	Jean Jenkins	4.50										
	June Bird	4.50										
15	Fred Wareham	4.50										
16	Ivy Jeans	4.50										
	Jill Stock	4.50	22.50		22.50							
			269.41		85.50			70.00		50.00	6.41	57.50

(b) Payments

Year 1	Detail	Total	Bank Contra	Printing & Stationery	Rent	Light & Heat	Postage	Sundries	Expenses re Dances	Expenses re Socials	Hon. Sec. Expenses	N.L.
	£	£	£	£	£	£	£	£	£	£	£	£
Jan. 4 David Parker – expenses re dance, deducted from proceeds (see debit entry £60.70)		9.30							9.30			
7 Party novelties for dance		14.65							14.65			
9 Pat Green – expenses for last year		27.46									27.46	
12 A.J.Smith – rent for January		25.00			25.00							
13 Electricity Board – quarter account		37.58				37.58						
14 Twangers Band – hire of band re dance		42.00							42.00			
17 Cash banked		100.00	100.00									
		255.99	100.00		25.00	37.58			65.95		27.46	

CHAPTER 4

Bank Reconciliations

Have you ever looked at your own Bank statement and been pleasantly surprised that it showed a reasonable sum in hand, only to get a rather shirty letter from your Bank manager a few days later. What has usually happened is that you have either forgotten that a cheque you had issued earlier had not been cleared, or that in carefully calculating your expenditure you had forgotten that a certain standing order had to be paid before the end of the month.

Such an experience is unpleasant to you and often to the manager, but he has a job to do which is to protect his customers' money and ensure that customers do not overdraw their accounts without prior authority. He is quite entitled to refuse to honour a cheque drawn on an account where the funds in hand are insufficient to meet the amount of the cheque. 'Refer to drawer' written in red ink on the top of the cheque which is returned to the payee does nothing for the drawer's reputation or image.

A Club Treasurer represents his organisation as one of its principal officers. If he is careless in issuing cheques which 'bounce' through lack of funds in the Bank account at the vital time, then that organisation's reputation suffers. Thus, it is absolutely vital to make sure that the entries in the club cash-book are reconciled monthly or weekly with the Bank statements. In this way he can be reasonably sure that he is fully aware of his Bank balance at any given moment.

The chance of the balance shown by his cash-book being exactly equal to the balance shown in the Bank statement is fairly small, although much will depend on the number of cheques paid out and the frequency of their issue. In the vast majority of cases, these are cheques which have been issued but which are still outstanding as they have not been received by the Bank for payment. This type of cheque is usually referred to as an *outstanding cheque.* Likewise, on the receipts side of the cash-book there may be cheques paid into the Bank account which have not yet appeared on the statement. For example, if you visit the Bank at 3.25 p.m. to pay in money and at the same time you ask for a copy of the Bank statement, then it would not be possible for that banking to appear on that statement. Cheques of this nature are referred to as *outstanding receipts* or *outstanding bankings.*

The task of 'reconciling' the cash-book and the Bank statements is largely a matter of procedure and technique which the Treasurer needs to know at the beginning of his term of office. For this reason the matter has been dealt with here in a separate chapter and full procedural details as well as practical examples with solutions have been provided. The best way to learn all book-keeping is to do plenty of worked examples rather than reading too many learned tomes.

The equipment you require to undertake a proper reconciliation are the cash-book, Bank statements made up to the latest possible date and a coloured pen or pencil. The latter is most helpful as will be seen in the course of this chapter, and if a different colour can be used each month, so much the better. The professional Accountant uses the different colours to enable him to rapidly distinguish the transactions each month. Thus cheques which are 'outstanding' and marked 'o/s' at the end of the month will appear in the Bank statement in the following month, but they are usually 'ticked' in the previous colour, showing clearly to which period they belong.

'Ticking' is a device which is widely used by Accountants when checking figures. One may use the traditional schoolteacher's type of 'tick' but some symbol is usually used that is restricted to a specific type of work. Thus, a letter 'B' may be used both in the Bank statement and in the cash-book to indicate that a figure appears in both places. With a little practice the Treasurer will be able to devise his own version.

There are several ways of starting, but the best is to work from the Bank statement to the cash-book. In this way, the Bank statement is made the master and the cash-book the slave. It is quite possible to work the other way round, but by using the method suggested you overcome the problem of being unable to alter the Bank's ledgers, whereas you can most certainly adjust your own cash-book. If you discover any errors in the statement, then it is simply a matter of asking the Bank to rectify them.

It is helpful to ensure that two tasks are completed before tackling the problem of the reconciliation process. First, ensure that the cash-book has been properly added up and a balance brought down. This speeds up the whole process and will make the task of reconciliation much more accurate, with the chance of obtaining an 'agreement' first time. The second task is to draft out a Bank reconciliation with sufficient space to ensure that entries can be made directly on to it. A typical lay-out will be as follows:

Bank Reconciliation

Balance per Bank statement (at the end of the period)
Add outstanding bankings   _____

Less outstanding cheques

Balance per cash-book   _____

The reconciliation is merely a list or statement showing the adjustment between the closing balance on the Bank statement and the cash-book balance, as amended by information obtained from the reconciliation process. It has nothing to do with a ledger account, and is prepared on a separate sheet of paper from the cash-book. At this stage a short example may be helpful, followed by a more detailed one later. The following figures are shown in the club cash-book and Bank statement respectively:

Cash-book

Debit		£	Credit		£
May 2	Balance b/f	450	May 4	MN	90
7	PQ Ltd	225	17	YZ	45
22	EF Ltd	51	27	MN	87
30	RT	117	30	Balance c/d	621
		£843			£843
May 30	Balance b/d	621			

Bank Statement for the month of May

		Debit £	Credit £	Balance £
May 2	Balance (credit)			450
7	PQ Ltd		225	675
11	MN	90		585
14	Credit transfer KL		48	633
24	EF		51	684
25	YZ	45		639
30	Bank charges	30		609

Check your efforts with the solution:

Cash-book

Debit		£			£
Balance b/f		621	May 30	Bank charges	30
May 14	Credit transfer KL	48	30	Balance c/d	639
		£669			£669
May 30	Balance b/d	639			

Bank Reconciliation

	£
Balance per Bank statement 30 May	609
Add outstanding banking	117
	726
Less outstanding cheques	87
Balance per cash-book	£639

When you come to do this task of reconciliation for the first time, there will seem to be a daunting number of different types of entries to deal with. The secret of success is to deal with one aspect at a time, and the reader is advised to repeat his efforts on the preceding example until he finds that he is quite familiar with the principles and techniques involved.

Unfortunately, not all Bank reconciliations are as straightforward as the last example. There is one complication to deal with, and that relates to cheques which are 'outstanding' from the previous period. These are payments made in the previous period but which have only come through the Bank statement in the current period. They were adjusted in the previous period's Bank reconciliation statement. Generally speaking, the correct treatment is to do nothing about them, but nevertheless they must be correctly identified.

The method of identifying and dealing with such 'outstandings' will become clearer after scrutinising the examples of the XYZ Club overleaf, and The Wealthy Society at the end of this chapter.

The reader is now invited to carry out the actual reconciliation process for himself using the following procedure.

It is helpful to start checking the items appearing in the 'Credit' column of the Bank statement with the corresponding debit items in the cash-book. The whole purpose of this procedure is to ensure that everything appearing in the Bank statement has its counterpart in the cash-book. If an item appears in the statement but not in the cash-book, it must be entered in the cash-book beneath the balance carried down.

The banking of £225 from PQ Ltd on 7 May is ticked with the corresponding item in the cash-book, likewise the £51. It seems that the credit transfer from KL of £48 shown on the statement is not reflected in the cash-book and must be entered beneath the balance carried down. The £48 on the Bank statement and £48 newly entered in the cash-book can now be 'ticked'.

At this stage the Accountant will ensure that all the Bank receipts have been ticked into the cash-book, and this is known as **clearing the entries**. If he is satisfied that all Bank entries are ticked, he passes on to the next stage.

It will be noticed that at this stage the £117 from RT appears as a receipt in the cash-book and is unticked. This indicates that for some reason it may either not have been paid into the account or that there has been a delay in its being credited to the Bank statement by the Bank. It should now be shown on the Bank reconciliation draft as an outstanding banking.

Having dealt with the Bank 'Credit' column, the 'Debit' column must be ticked in a similar manner. The cheque for £90 to MN on the statement is ticked against that in the cash-book, and likewise the £45 to YZ. Bank charges of £30 are shown on the Bank statement, but these are not reflected in the cash-book, and must now be entered as a payment in the cash-book, and can be ticked.

The Accountant will 'clear through the entries' on the debit side of the Bank statement to ensure that they are fully ticked. If satisfied that this is so, he then lists as 'outstanding cheques' on the Bank reconciliation draft, those cheques appearing unticked in the cash-book. The cheque for £87 payable to MN is the only one in this example.

The closing balance in the Bank statement, £609, is also entered in the Bank reconciliation draft and the additions on the draft and the amended cash-book are completed. The result will be that the new balance in the cash-book exactly equals that shown in the Bank reconciliation draft.

Example

XYZ CLUB

Cash-book of XYZ Club for the month of October

			£				£
Oct.	1	Balance b/f	872	Oct.	6	Pink	458
	2	Red	108		20	Brown	315
	4	Blue	249		27	Magenta	160
	6	Green	265		28	Orange	138
	9	Black	158		29	Tangerine	13
							1084
	16	Yellow	148				
	23	Purple	76		31	Balance c/d	966
	29	White	174				
			£2050				£2050
Oct. 31		Balance b/d	966				

Bank Statements for the month of October

			Payments £	Receipts £	Balance £
Oct.	1	Balance b/f			1008
	2	Credit		108	1116
	7	Credit		514	1630
	10	Auburn	136		1494
	11	Credit		158	1652
	11	Pink	458		1194
	16	Credit		148	1342
	23	Credit		76	1418
	23	Brown	315		1103
	29	Bank charges	57		1046

Solution

Cash-book of XYZ Club for month of October

			£		£
Oct.	31	Balance b/f	966	Bank charges	57
				Balance c/d	909
			£966		£966
Oct.	31	Balance b/d	909		

Bank Reconciliation

	£	£
Balance per Bank statement – 31 October		1046
Add outstanding bankings – white		174
		1220
Less outstanding cheques – Magenta	160	
Orange	138	
Tangerine	13	311
Balance per cash-book		£909

As before, we start by working from the Receipts column of the Bank statement into the receipts side of the cash-book. In order to make the sequence of events clear, they are tabulated below with an explanation of each stage where necessary:

(1) The entries of £108 correspond and are ticked.

(2) The cash-book shows receipt on 4 October of £249 and £265 on 6 October, while the Bank statement only shows a figure of £514 on 7 October. It is apparent that in total the cash-book and the statement agree, so again the entries may be ticked. This situation will frequently be found in book-keeping as receipts will be received by a club or organisation daily, but there may be a lapse of several days before these are paid into the Bank. The Bank is merely interested in the total paid in. Full details of the make-up of each banking will, of course, be shown in the customer's copy of the pay-in book.

(3) The £158, £148 and £76 have their counterpart in each place and are ticked off.

(4) The Receipts column of the Bank statement can be ticked at the top to indicate that it has to be 'cleared' and no more items have to be dealt with.

(5) The payments side of the statement must now be approached in a similar manner. The statement shows £136 paid to Auburn on 10 October, and appears to have no corresponding entry in the payments side of the cash-book. Following the procedure already laid down for missing items, it would seem sensible to enter this on the payments side of the cash-book. Beware, the £136 is an example of an 'outstanding' cheque from the month of September. If you had available the September Bank reconciliation, you could verify that fact. In this example it is also possible to show them by a simple statement:

	£
Balance per Bank statement October	1008
Less outstanding cheque from September	136
Balance brought forward in cash-book	£872

Having established beyond doubt that it is an 'outstanding' cheque, all that need be done is to tick the entry on the Bank statement with that shown in the September Bank reconciliation. Make sure, in due course, that all the September outstanding cheques have come through in October. If they are still outstanding at the end of October, you must include them as outstanding in your October reconciliation.

(6) The payments of £458 and £315 may be ticked as corresponding.

(7) The Bank charges of £57 must be entered as a payment in the cash-book.

(8) Tick the top of the payments column of the Bank statement as this is now cleared.

(9) Enter the closing balance on the Bank statement of £1046 into the Bank reconciliation.

(10) Any unticked items on the receipts side of the cash-book should be listed as outstanding banking on the reconciliation. In this case, there is only the £174.

(11) List the unticked payments in the cash-book and insert as outstanding cheques in the reconciliation. In our example the three cheques total £311.

(12) Complete the additions in the cash-book and the reconciliation. The balances should agree. If the balances do not agree, then obviously there is an error, and the following procedure should be followed to trace the problem:

    (i) If there is an overdraft involved, the *Add* and *Less* on the reconciliation layout may have to be reversed. (See the following RST Social Club exercise and the note thereto.)

    (ii) Ensure that all the payments and bankings shown as 'Outstanding' in the previous month's reconciliation have either been traced through the Bank statements or are carried forward in the current month's reconciliation.

    (iii) Examine the Bank statements to see whether any entry has not been ticked.

    (iv) Check the additions of the cash-book and check the balance carried forward.

    (v) If none of these methods reveal the error, repeat the original 'ticking' procedure, using a different colour or an ordinary pencil. This will make it easier to see the difference between the two efforts.

Exercise

R. S. T. SOCIAL CLUB

The Club Treasurer is unable to understand why the Bank statement shows an overdraft at the end of May when he endeavours to keep a credit balance with the Bank at all times. All payments are made by cheque and all receipts banked. Having some knowledge of book-keeping, you offer to assist. Prepare the amended cash-book entries and the Bank reconciliation.

Lender Bank Ltd – Bank Statement

		Payments £	Receipts £	Balance £
May 1	Balance b/f			367 Cr.
6	Credits		159	526 Cr.
13	Credits		587	1113 Cr.
14	Fags Ltd	342		771 Cr.
19	Credits		43	814 Cr.
20	Brewery Ltd	462		352 Cr.
26	Credits		311	663 Cr.
27	Sports Ltd	381		282 Cr.
28	Standing order	35		247 Cr.
29	Cheque returned	311		64 Dr.
31	Credits		42	22 Dr.

Cash-book

			£				£
May	1	Balance b/f	25	May	5	Brewery Ltd	452
	3	Subscriptions	70		19	Sports Ltd	381
	5	Subscriptions	89		26	Tobacco Ltd	94
	6	Bar takings	347		27	Cleaner	21
	11	Bar takings	240		29	Booze Ltd	118
	18	Subscriptions	43				1066
	25	Mr Broke – half-year's rent	311			Balance c/d	485
	30	Bar takings	384				
	31	Subscriptions	42				
			£1551				£1551
May	31	Balance b/d	485				

Suggested solution

R.S.T. SOCIAL CLUB

(a)

Cash-book

			£			£
May 31	Balance b/d	485		Brewery Ltd re error (£462 − 452)		10
				Standing order		35
				Mr Broke, cheque returned unpaid		331
						376
				Balance c/d		109
			£485			£485
May 31	Balance b/d	109				

(b)

Bank Reconciliation

		£	£
Balance per Bank statement 31 May			42 Dr.
Add outstanding bankings			384
			342
Less outstanding cheques:	Tobacco	94	
	Cleaner	21	
	Booze	118	233
Balance per cash-book			£109

Note

The effect of paying £384 into the Bank account which was overdrawn to the extent of £42, is to turn the overdraft to a positive figure. However, if the outstanding banking is less than the overdraft shown by the Bank statement, both the *Add* and *Less* signs must be reversed.

33

Example

THE WEALTHY SOCIETY
Cash-book

			£					£	
Aug.	1	Balance b/f	8246	Aug.	1	Cheque	951	429	
	2	Takings	481		6	„	952	110	
	3	„	551		13	„	953	256	
	11	„	1156		18	„	954	49	
	15	„	209		20	„	955	171	
	20	„	163		29	„	956	130	
	25	„	265					1145	
	30	„	60			Balance c/d		9986	
			£11131					£11131	
Aug. 31		Balance b/d	9986						

Secure Bank Ltd
Bank Statement – The Wealthy Society

			Payments £	Receipts £	Balance £
Aug.	1	Balance b/f			8739
	2	949	213		8526
	3	Remittance		88	8614
	6	951	429		8185
	6	Charges	23		8162
	7	950	368		7794
	7	Counter credit		1032	8826
	9	Standing order	68		8758
	12	952	106		8652
	13	Remittance		1156	9808
	16	953	256		9552
	16			209	9761
	21	Remittance		163	9924
	25	Counter Credit		264	10188
	26	955	171		10017
	29	427	148		9869

August Bank Reconciliation

	£	£
Balance per Bank statement		
31 August		9869
Add outstanding banking		60
		9929
Less outstanding cheques	49	
	130	179
Balance per cash-book		
31 August		£9750

34

		£		£
Aug. 31	Balance b/f	9986	Adjustment re error in banking (265 − 264)	1
	Adjustment re cheque 952 (£110 − 106)	4	Charges	23
			Standing order	68
			Cheque 427	148
			(Query if debited in error by Bank)	
				240
			Balance c/d	9750
		£9990		£9990
	Balance b/d	9750		

Note

The balance in the cash-book at 1 August is made up as follows:

	£	£
Bank balance 1 August		8739
Add outstanding receipt		88
		8827
Less outstanding cheques	213	
	368	581
		£8246

CHAPTER 5

The Final Accounts

In Chapter 1 the reader was made aware of the two types of final accounts. Either the Summary Receipts and Payments account is used or the more comprehensive Income and Expenditure account with attached Balance Sheet, and much will depend on the club's requirements. For the very small club or social group the former is usually sufficient, although it is useful to attach additional information such as the amount of unpaid bills or members' subscriptions which have been received in advance. The Treasurer does not require any special skills, and reference should be made to Schedules (C) and (E) of the Frendlee Club example in the Appendix.

At this point the faint-hearted Treasurer may wish to 'shut off' and put the book down, rejoicing that for his purpose the Receipts and Payments account is sufficient. However, the braver reader should read on – the rewards in terms of personal satisfaction will be considerable. To have produced a full Income and Expenditure account with Balance Sheet will be rather like making something, or on a par with an artist creating a picture. There is a sense of purpose and achievement.

There are two systems for the preparation of the final accounts; both will be described in detail. The Treasurer must decide in the light of the circumstances which method is appropriate for his purposes. As a general guide, the larger and more complex organisation will require a ledger in addition to the analysed cash-book, as this will in the end simplify matters although it will initially involve more book-keeping.

The Ledger System

The Treasurer of any large club is almost bound to need a ledger in addition to his analysed cash-book. The purpose of the ledger is to enable income and expenditure to be analysed as it is incurred, and to fully record the assets and liabilities of the organisation. It is the inability of the cash-book to record these that makes the ledger desirable, especially if the organisation owns any reasonable quantity of assets.

Each ledger account will be ruled as a 'T' account and will look like a Cash account. Normally there will be no analysis columns on the ledger account although such things do exist especially in some systems of loose-leaf ledgers. These 'exotic' things are best ignored by the Treasurer as they will merely be an additional and needless complication.

At this stage the reader needs to learn two more technical words. Accountants talk of **casting** and **posting**. 'Casting the books' or 'doing the casts' merely means adding them up. 'Posting' means the completion of the double entry of a transaction. Thus, the original entry in the cash-book will be completed by being posted or entered in the appropriate ledger account.

The Treasurer, acting as book-keeper, must first 'post up' his cash-book and ledger before preparing the trial balance. Then, acting as an Accountant, he will close off the ledger accounts to the Income and Expenditure account as he goes through the ledger. Any ledger accounts left open will appear in the Balance Sheet.

Reference should now be made to Schedule (H) in the Appendix. These are the completed ledger accounts for the Frendlee Club.

The procedure for opening up a ledger is to have a statement of affairs at the commencement if no Balance Sheet is available for this purpose. In the Frendlee Club case the statement of affairs is shown in Schedule (B) in the Appendix. This is simply a list of the assets and liabilities at the commencement of the period, and the balance on the Accumulated Fund is merely the difference between the two sides. This enables the book-keeping to be commenced with books which balance, rather like a trial balance, but remember, prior to the statement of affairs there was no double entry in evidence. This is the whole purpose of preparing the statement of affairs.

A separate ledger account is then opened for each item appearing in the statement of affairs, and the balance will be transferred to each ledger account on the same side as it appears on the statement of affairs. Thus, the games equipment of £1535 appears on the debit side of the Games Equipment account. To ensure that the reader understands the procedure, he should now 'tick' entries from the statement of affairs into the ledger accounts, not forgetting that the Bank balance will be shown in the cash-book.

The next stage is to post up the totals and analysed figures from the cash-book into the ledger. This should be done direct from the cash-book rather than from the medium of a summary Bank account such as Schedule (C) in the Appendix. Merely for the sake of convenience, at this point it is probably easier to 'tick' from the ledger accounts back into the cash-book, care being taken to ensure that the double entry is fully understood in each case.

Certain accounts will require adjustment. For example, there is a creditor for £13.47 on the Stationery account as at 30 September Year 2. This is effected by debiting the current period of the accounts and then carrying it down as a credit balance. The credit balance clearly indicates a creditor, and will be shown under the heading of 'current liabilities' in the Balance Sheet.

In contrast, there is a prepayment of £14.60 on the Insurance account. This means that part of the payments of £176 refers to the following period. The effect of the entry is to reduce the expense for the year, and the amount carried forward is treated as a current asset in the Balance Sheet.

The reader should 'tick' these adjustments, including the stock of food. First 'tick' the double entry on the face of the ledger account, i.e. the bringing down of the balance, creditor or stock. Then 'tick' it into the Balance Sheet under the headings 'current liabilities' or 'current assets'.

The final step in the preparation of the accounts is to 'tick' the transfers to the Income and Expenditure account and also to the Balance Sheet.

When the Treasurer actually comes to do the task himself he will need to ensure that all entries from the cash book have been posted into the ledger. Usually there is a reference made to the number of the cash-book page in the ledger account and the number of the ledger account in the cash-book.

Next, it is very helpful to have a draft set of final accounts ready. This is a copy of the Income and Expenditure account with no figures except comparative ones. Comparative figures are those relating to the previous year and are normally shown in the left-hand margin of both Income and Expenditure and Balance Sheet. Some companies publish their annual accounts with the figures for the preceding year alongside the current year, perhaps using a different colour to make them clearer. Since most club accounts are simple and are shown in black and white rather than colour, the left-hand margin convention is perhaps a useful one as members cannot confuse the figures for the current and past year's performance.

Armed with a draft set of accounts, the Treasurer can set about the task of filling in the various sections as he goes through the ledger. This avoids the need to go through the ledger twice, first for the Income and Expenditure account and then for the Balance Sheet.

In transferring items to the Income and Expenditure account, make sure that the ledger account is properly ruled off, with double lines beneath the total figures. As with balancing a Cash account, keep ledger account totals on the same level. Failure to do this, or not to use the double lines, can lead to confusion and error in the following period. It is easy to add into the figures of a current period those relating to the previous year and not clearly dealt with at that time. As with most procedures and practices in life there is a good reason for their existence. The reason for Income and Expenditure ledger accounts being ruled off is that the life of such accounts is limited to one year at a time, in contrast to Balance Sheet items such as fixed assets where existence continues year by year.

When the Income and Expenditure account has been completed, the Balance Sheet can then be prepared. Notice that an excess of receipts over payments for the year is added to the Accumulated Fund, whilst the reverse is true.

Layout is a matter of choice. Some feel the conventional side-by-side layout of the Income and Expenditure account and Balance Sheet easiest to understand, but the trend is for vertical accounting. The two contrasting styles can be seen in the Frendlee Club example, Schedules (F) and (G) in the Appendix.

Preparation of Final Accounts from Incomplete Records

(1) The schedule system

The headache of many practising Accountants is what is known as **incomplete records**. These are accounting records, usually of receipts and payments of cash and/or cheques, where the double entry has not been completed. Unfortunately, many small traders have records in this category and the sorting-out process is long-winded and the end-product is not always very satisfactory. However, where the Cash and Bank accounts are properly kept, especially on the analysis system, the completion of the double entry is not too difficult and proper accounts can be reasonably quickly prepared. The method used is largely one of technique.

One such method is to adopt the system used by Accountants as laid out in Schedule (J), the Frendlee Club example in the Appendix. It is useful because it can deal with complex problems, and each stage of the work can be arithmetically proved. This applies vertically and horizontally.

A sheet of analysis paper should be headed in the manner shown in Schedule (J). If needed, additional columns can be added, but normally the only reason for doing this would be for the inclusion of another Bank account; then the Deposit account could be treated in this way if desired.

The first task is to ensure that the opening balances are fully entered in the schedule. These figures are taken either from the previous Balance Sheet or, in the case of a club preparing accounts for the first time, on a double-entry basis from a statement of affairs. When the figures are fully entered, check that the totals balance.

Next, enter the Bank summary. If the reader compares the totals shown on the Schedule (J) with the Bank summary, Schedule (C) he will probably feel that a mistake has been made in the example, as the columns seem to have become reversed. The receipts shown in the Bank summary, which were on the debit side, now appear in the credit column in the schedule. There is a reason for this. For practical convenience, the two Bank columns on Schedule (J) are reversed so that they give the effect of the double entry being completed. At this stage no double entry has been completed but it assists the Accountant to do so. In other words, figures now appear to be on their correct sides even if strictly this is not true. Perhaps this is most clearly shown by an example. Under the heading 'Members' Subscriptions', the £991.50 correctly appears on the credit side, indicating the side that one might expect it to be on if the double entry were completed in a ledger account. Since there is already £45 brought forward from the previous period as a credit balance, indicating that subscriptions relating to the current year had been received in the former period, this must be added to the £991.50 to give £1036.50 to be entered in the credit column of the Income and Expenditure account in due course.

Having explained why the Bank columns are entered in this 'backwards' manner, the Treasurer should now ensure that, as far as possible, any receipts and payments which relate to items listed from the previous Balance Sheet or statement of affairs are entered against those items. Thus £176 for insurance was entered opposite the £11 prepayment brought forward, while the £76.79 paid for Treasurer's expenses was put on the same line as the £19 creditor. While it is most convenient to make entries in this way, the adjustment columns can be used to transfer information from other parts of the schedule to their proper location. Take, for example, the second instance of item 'Records & tapes' in the schedule. By putting £148.05 on the credit side of the adjustment column and debiting 'Records & tapes' at its first instance in the schedule, opposite the £160 brought forward, the problem of having two separate lines for 'Records & tapes' is avoided.

When the Bank receipts and payments have been allied, check that the totals agree with the Bank summary.

The reader may wonder about the purpose of the 'adjustment' columns. As in the case of the £148.05 for the 'Records & tapes', they enable errors in analysis to be corrected, and they also show the double-entry aspect of certain transactions. The £270 which is an addition to the 'Amplifier & equipment' is also a creditor. This equipment was purchased before the Balance Sheet date but paid for afterwards. By debiting the adjustment account and crediting the Balance Sheet credit column the double entry is completed and the two aspects of the transaction are clearly recorded. In addition, their accuracy can now be proved horizontally by looking at the £1120 and £270 on the Balance Sheet debit and credit columns respectively.

The method of proceeding is to start from the top of the first page of the schedule, working through each item line by line. Normally each line will appear in either the Income and Expenditure and/or the Balance Sheet. Some items cancel themselves out but are still included in the final accounts for information. Receipts re 'Visits by members' and the 'Members Xmas lunch' are in this category.

When each line is completed, add both columns of the Income and Expenditure. The difference is the 'Profit or Loss' arising. In the example the difference is £218.31 representing an excess of expenditure over income for the period. Notice at the foot of Schedule (J) how the difference is inserted under the debit column of the balance Sheet column so that when those sides are added they agree at £6046.88.

The final accounts can now be written up from the completed schedule.

(2) An alternative

Accountants tend to prefer the schedule system as it is more in keeping with their traditional method of preparing accounts and it will also help in complex cases. However, the average Club Treasurer may prefer to use a less formal system, provided he is able to understand the basic system of double-entry book-keeping.

Example

THE SOCIAL CLUB

The Club Treasurer decided to prepare an Income and Expenditure account and Balance Sheet for the year ended 31 December Year 4, in addition to his usual Receipts and Payments account. By doing so he felt that members could be given more information about the Club's financial position. He extracted the following details from the books of the Club.

Position as at 1 January Year 4	£
Cash at Bank	326
Cash in Hand	62
Furniture & sports equipment	320
Subscriptions due from members for Year 3	34
Subscriptions paid in advance for Year 4	20

Receipts and Payments during the year were summarised as follows:	£
Additional chairs	140
Subscriptions received (including £34 for Year 3 and £30 for Year 5)	284
Profit from whist drives, etc.	96
Rent	120
Repairs to equipment	8
Gas & electricity	18
Cleaning	48
Honorarium to officials	40
Postage & stationery	10

At the end of the year (31 December Year 4) Subscriptions in arrear were £46, and of the money held by the Club £32 was in cash and the remainder in the Bank. One quarter's rent of £24 had been paid in advance and there was an account owing in respect of repairs to table-tennis equipment amounting to £6. Furniture and sports equipment is to be depreciated by 10 per cent.

THE SOCIAL CLUB

Suggested solution

(a)   Statement of Affairs at 1 January Year 4

	Dr.	Cr.
	£	£
Cash at Bank	326	
Cash in Hand	62	
Furniture & sports equipment	320	
Subscriptions due from members for Year 3	34	
Subscriptions paid in advance for Year 4		20
Accumulated Fund		722
	£742	£742

(*Note* – The amount of £722 on the Accumulated account is simply a balancing figure inserted into the Statement of Affairs so that the following book-keeping can be based on accounts that balance.)

(b)

Summary Receipts & Payments Account
for the Year ended 31 December Year 4

	£	£		£	£
Balances brought forward			Additional chairs		140
1 January:			Rent		120
Cash at Bank	326		Repairs to equipment		8
Cash in Hand	62	388	Gas & electricity		18
Subscriptions received for			Cleaning		48
Yr 3	34		Postage & stationery		10
Yr 4	220		Honorarium to official		40
Yr 5	30	284	Balances carried forward		
Profit from whist drives, etc.		96	31 December:		
			Cash at Bank	352	
			Cash in Hand	32	384
		£768			£768

(c)

Income and Expenditure Account
for the Year ended 31 December Year 4

	£		£
Rent (120 − 24)	96	Subscriptions received	286
Repairs to equipment (8 + 6)	14	Profit from whist drives, etc.	96
Gas & electricity	18		
Cleaning	48		
Postage & stationery	10		
Honorarium to official	40		
Depreciation on furniture & sports equipment at 10%	46		
	272		
Excess of Income over Expenditure for the year	110		
	£382		£382

Working Note

Subscriptions Account

			£				£		£
Jan.	1	Subs. due re Yr 3	34	Jan.	1	Subs. in advance re Yr 4			20
Dec.	31	Transfer I. & E. A/c	286	Dec.	31	Receipts & Payments A/c			
„	31	Subs. in advance				re Yr 3	34		
		re Yr 5	c/d	30		Yr 4	220		
						Yr 5	30	284	
				„	31	Debtors re Subs. due			
						re Yr 4, unpaid	c/d	46	
			£350					£350	
Dec.	31	Debtors re Yr 4	b/d	46	Dec.	31	Subs. re Yr 5	b/d	30

Accumulated Fund	£	£	*Furniture & Sports Equipment*	£	£
Balance brought forward		722	Balance brought forward		
1 January			1 January		320
Add Excess of Income over Ex-			Additions during the year		140
penditure for the year		110			460
		832	*Less* depreciation for the year		46
Current Liabilities					414
Creditors	6				
Subscriptions in advance	30	36			
			Current Assets		
			Cash at Bank	352	
			Cash in Hand	32	
			Subscriptions due	46	
			Prepayment	24	454
		£868			£868

The example of The Social Club attempts to show how a reasonably straightforward set of accounts can be prepared without the use of either a ledger or the schedule system. It is assumed, however, that the cash-book has been properly kept and that the Treasurer is able to produce a summary Bank/Cash account.

Where there is no prior Balance Sheet available, the first step is to produce a statement of affairs as in (a) in the suggested solution. As is said in the note in the illustration, the figure shown for the Accumulated Fund is merely the balancing figure, being the difference between the totals of the debit and credit columns. As always, the purpose of the statement of affairs is to provide a base on which to build the subsequent book-keeping.

Next, a summary Receipts and Payments account for the period is prepared. It will be noted in the example that both cash and Bank items are shown on the one account. This is simply the aggregation of the separate Cash and Bank accounts, although it may be better to keep the accounts separate if an Income and Expenditure account is to be prepared for publication.

The main points to note about the summary Receipts and Payments account are that the opening cash/Bank balances will appear in the statement of affairs, while the closing balances will appear under the heading of 'Current Assets' in the Balance Sheet. When the summary is used to prepare an Income and Expenditure account, the double entry will be completed by posting the items to the opposite sides. Thus the credit entry of £48 for cleaning in the summary will appear as a debit, being an expense, on the Income and Expenditure account. Similarly, the £96 profit on the dances becomes a credit in the Income and Expenditure account.

In preparing the Income and Expenditure account, brackets have been used to show the adjustments made to certain receipts and payments. Three of these items need explanation.

The question states that one-quarter's rent had been paid in advance so that £24 of the £120 related to the three months of January to March in Year 5. Thus, it is necessary to take out this item and show it as a prepayment under 'Current Assets' in the Balance Sheet. Technically, the £24 would be carried down as a debit balance on the face of the Rent account if a proper ledger account had been maintained.

In contrast to the situation where the rent was reduced, in the case of the repairs to equipment, there is still a bill for £6 to be paid. Thus, the true cost of equipment repairs for the year must be that which has already been paid, plus the creditor of £6. The word 'creditor' is also a reminder that a transaction is viewed from two points of view. Not only is the £6 bill an expense, but it is also a creditor. The corresponding credit entry is therefore under the heading of 'Current Liabilities' in the Balance Sheet.

Of all the adjustments, the most complex in the question was that of the figure for subscriptions. The principle which underlies these adjustments is that an expense or a profit or gain should be shown in the Income and Expenditure account only if it relates to the exact period covered by that account. Anything else is excluded.

The Income and Expenditure figure for subscriptions can be reconciled as under the following:

		£	£
Year 3			
	Subscriptions due to Club	34	
	Less paid in Year 4	34	—
Year 4			
	Subscriptions – paid in advance	20	
	– received during year	220	
	– due but unpaid at year end (i.e. debtors)	46	
			286
Year 5			
	Subscriptions received during the year	30	
	Less carried forward under current liabilities	30	
		—	—
	Per Income and Expenditure account		£286

A necessary adjustment to the Income and Expenditure is the inclusion of depreciation to the fixed asset of furniture and sports equipment. Note that the asset figure of £320 is a debit balance to which is added the £140 for additional chairs. It is on the total figure of £460 that the 10 per cent depreciation is calculated. The double entry for depreciation is to debit the Income and Expenditure account and credit the asset account.

The additions are now completed in the Income and Expenditure account, the balance being added or deducted from the Accumulated Fund which in turn enables the Balance Sheet to be completed.

The reader is invited to 'tick' through the solution to ensure that the principles are fully understood, and then to work the following exercises:

44

(a) The Get Weaving Society
(b) The Play Reading Society
(c) The Topers Club

Exercise

THE GET WEAVING SOCIETY

Last year the Members of the Society protested to the Treasurer that a Receipts and Payments account did not clearly show the financial position of the Society. The Treasurer was requested to prepare an Income and Expenditure account for the current year ended 30 September Year 9, with a Balance Sheet as at that date.

The assets of the Society at 30 September Year 8 were a balance on Current account £233 and Cash in Hand £28.

The following receipts and payments for the year ended 30 September Year 9 were extracted from the Treasurer's cash-book.

Receipts	£	£	Payments	£
Subscriptions – Yr 8	188		Visiting speakers & courses	424
– Yr 9	48		Books	26
		236	Secretarial expenses	66
Charges to members re courses &			Society's magazine	53
speakers		223	Transfers to Deposit account	375
Transfers from Deposit account		325	Purchase of fleeces	24
Sale of Society's magazine		43	Printing & stationery	4
Donation received		3	Subscriptions	8
Miscellaneous receipts		9		
Sale of fleeces		10		

Cash in Hand at 30 September Year 9 amounted to £18. Interest of £6 had been received in the Bank Deposit account during the year. There was an unpaid bill for secretarial expenses of £5.

Suggested solution

THE GET WEAVING SOCIETY

(a)

Statement of Affairs as at 30 September Year 8

	Dr.	Cr.
Bank Current account	£233	
Cash in Hand	28	
Accumulated Fund		261
	£261	261

(b)

Income and Expenditure Account for the Year ended 30 September Year 9

	£	£		£
Courses and speakers	424		Subscriptions (236 − 48)	188
Less Receipts from members	223		Donation received	3
	—	201	Interest on Bank deposit	6
Books		26	Miscellaneous receipt	9
Secretarial expenses (66 + 5)		71	Excess of Expenditure over Income for	
Society's magazine	53		the year	128
Less Sales to members	43			
	—	10		
Purchase of fleeces	24			
Less Sales to members	10			
	—	14		
Subscription		8		
Printing & stationery		4		
		£334		£334

(c)

Balance Sheet as at 30 September Year 9

Accumulated Fund	£	£	*Current Assets*	£
Balance as at 30 September Yr 8		261	Bank – Current A/c	112
			– Deposit A/c	56
Less Excess of Expenditure over			Cash in Hand	18
Income for the year		128		
		133		
Current Liabilities				
Creditor	5			
Prepayment of next year's				
subscriptions	48	53		
		£186		£186

(d)

Cash and Bank Summary for the Year ended 30 September Year 9

	£	£		£	£
Balances at 30 September Yr 8			Purchase of fleeces		24
Bank	233		Printing & stationery		4
Cash	28		Visiting speakers & courses		424
	—	261	Books		26
Subscription – Yr 8	188		Secretarial expenses		66
do. Yr 9	48		Society's purchase of magazine		53
	—	236	Transfer to Deposit A/c		375
Charges to members re courses			Subscriptions		8
& speakers		223			
Sale of Society's magazine		43			
Transfer from Deposit A/c		325			
Donation received		3	Balances at 30 September Yr 9		
Miscellaneous receipts		9	Bank	112	
Sales of fleeces		10	Cash	18	130
		£1110			£1110

46

(e)

Bank – Deposit Account

		£
Receipts		375
Less Payments		325
		50
Add Interest received during the year		6
Balance at 30 September Yr 9		£56

Exercise

THE PLAY READING SOCIETY

From the following Receipts and Payments account and notes relating to the Play Reading Society, you are required to prepare an Income and Expenditure account for the year ended 30 September Year 2, and a Balance Sheet as at that date.

Receipts and Payments Account for the
Year ended 30 September Year 2

	£		£
Balance 30 September Yr 1	48	Wages	200
Subscriptions	642	Stationery	86
Donations received	20	New equipment	104
		Printing	140
		Catering expenses	68
		Balance 30 September Yr 2	112
	£710		£710

At 30 September Year 1 the Society's equipment was valued at £296, subscriptions in arrear were £54 and there were creditors for catering provisions of £12. At 30 September Year 2 subscriptions in arrear amounted to £30 and subscriptions in advance were £18. There were creditors for printing £6 and catering provisions £10. The Society had a stock of stationery valued at £16. The sum of £40 is to be provided for depreciation of equipment.

Suggested solution

THE PLAY READING SOCIETY

(a)

Statement of Affairs as at 30 September Year 1

	Dr.	Cr.
	£	£
Cash/Bank	48	
Equipment	296	
Subscriptions re Year 1	54	
Creditor for catering provisions		12
Accumulated Fund		386
	£398	£398

(b)
Income and Expenditure Account for the Year ended 30 September Year 2

	£		£
Wages	200	Subscriptions (642 − 54 + 30 − 18)	600
Stationery (86 − 16)	70	Donations received	20
Printing (140 + 6)	146		
Catering expenses (68 − 12 + 10)	66		
Depreciation of equipment	40		
	522		
Excess of Income over Expenditure for the year	98		
	£620		£620

(c)
Balance Sheet as at 30 September Year 2

Accumulated Fund	£	£	Fixed Assets	£	£
Balance at 30 September Yr 1		386	Equipment at 30 September Yr 1		296
Add Excess of Income over Expenditure for the year		98	Additions during the year		104
					400
		484	*Less* Depreciation @ 10%		40
					360
Current Liabilities			Current Assets		
Creditors (6 + 10)	16		Cash/Bank	112	
Subscriptions in advance	18		Stock of stationery	16	
	—	34	Debtor – subscriptions	30	158
		£518			£518

Exercise

THE TOPERS CLUB

The Topers Club prepares its annual accounts to 30 June in each year. The summarised Balance Sheet as at 30 June Year 6 showed the following position:

	£		£
Accumulated Fund	7286	Fixtures & fittings	1920
Expenses accrued – Heat & light	63	Bar stock	1101
do. – Bar purchases	250	Prepayment – rates	69
		Balance at Bank	4176
		Cash in Hand	333
	£7599		£7599

The part-time book-keeper prepared a summary of the Receipts and Payments for the year ended 30 June Year 7 as follows:

	£		£	£
Balance at Bank 30 June		Bar purchases		24492
Yr 6 – Current A/c	4176	Wages – Bar Steward	2144	
Cash in Hand 30 June Yr 6	333	do. – Part-time book-		
Subscriptions	2760	keeper	300	
Bar receipts	31200	do. – Cleaner	400	
Loans from members	15000			2844
Catering receipts	1620	Heating & lighting		438
		Rent & rates		921
		Postage & stationery		207
		Catering purchases		1020
		Purchase of Clubhouse		
		freehold		15000
		General expenses		450
		Repairs & maintenance		606
		Repayment of members' loans		1500
		Balance at Bank 30 June Yr 7:		
		Current A/c	1236	
		Deposit A/c	6000	
				7236
		Cash in hand 30 June Yr 7		375
	£55089			£55089

During the year, the Club decided to purchase the freehold of the Clubhouse from the landlord for £15,000. The transaction was financed by interest-free loans from Members as the Club had insufficient cash resources. The sum of £1500 is to be repaid each year to Members selected by an annual draw, and the Finance Committee felt that an equal amount should be charged in the annual accounts and credited to a separate reserve.

At the request of Members, the Bar Steward had started providing snacks in the bar and it had been agreed that provision should be made for a bonus to him of 50 per cent of the gross profit on the catering venture.

The book-keeper states that at 30 June Year 7 the bar stock was £1293 and that there were creditors for bar purchases of £275 and electricity £51. Rates were prepaid to the extent of £75. Depreciation on fixtures & fittings is to be provided at the rate of 10 per cent per annum on the reducing balance.

As Treasurer, you are asked to prepare the Income and Expenditure account for the year ended 30 June Year 7, and a Balance Sheet at that date.

Suggested solution

THE TOPERS CLUB

(a)

Bar and Catering Accounts for the Year ended 30 June Year 7

	£	Bar £	Catering £
Takings		31200	1620
Opening stock	1101		
Purchases (24492 − 250 + 275)	24517		1020
	25618		
Less closing stock	1293		
	24325		
Bar Steward's wages	2144	26469	
Gross profit carried to Income and Expenditure account		£4731	£600

(b)

Income and Expenditure Account for the Year ended 30 June Year 7

Income	£	£	£
Subscriptions			2760
Gross profit on bar			4731
Gross profit on catering		600	
Less bonus to Steward		300	300
			7791

Expenditure	£	£	£
Establishment Costs			
Rent & rates (921 + 69 − 75)	915		
Heating & lighting (438 − 63 + 51)	426		
Repairs & maintenance	606		
Depreciation of fixtures & fittings @ 10%	192		
	—	2139	
Administrative & General Costs			
Wages & National Insurance (400 + 300)	700		
Postage and stationery	207		
General expenses	450	1357	3496
			4295
Net Surplus on General Account			
Less transfer to reserve of amount equal to loan repayments during the year			1500
Net surplus carried to Accumulated Fund			£2795

(c)

Balance Sheet as at 30 June Year 7

Capital Employed

	£	£
Accumulated Fund		
Balance at 30 June Year 6		7286
Add surplus for the year		2795
		10081
Loan Repayment Reserve		1500
Members Loan		
Amount advanced	15000	
Less repaid during year	1500	13500
		£25081

Represented by:

	£	£	£
Fixed Assets			
Freehold Clubhouse, at cost			15000
Fixtures & fittings, less depreciation (1920 – 192)			1728
			16728
Net Current Assets			
Bar stock		1293	
Repayments		75	
Cash at Bank – Current account		1236	
– Deposit account		6000	
Cash in Hand		375	
		8979	
Less Accrued Expenses (275 + 51)	326		
Bonus to Steward	300	626	8353
			£25081

(*Note* – The figures in brackets are only for the purpose of this illustration so that the reader can see how they are computed. They should not be shown on accounts submitted to members of a club.)

CHAPTER 6

Points to Consider

Subscriptions

In The Social Club example beginning on page 41, the Subscriptions account was examined in some detail, and the actual ledger account is shown as a working note below the Income and Expenditure account in the illustration.

In considering this topic, it is essential to remember that when an Income and Expenditure account is prepared, the Treasurer is only concerned with bringing in the actual subscriptions, either received or which shall have been received during the period covered by the account. Normally it will be for one year, neither more nor less.

The Income and Expenditure account of the Social Club is for the year ended 31 December Year 4. Although the Treasurer had received late subscriptions for Year 3 during the early part of the year, and some for Year 5 in advance at the end of the year, receipts for both Years 3 and 5 must be eliminated from our Income and Expenditure for Year 4. In our example, £34 was due in respect of Year 3 at the beginning of Year 4, and as this amount was received during the year the net effect was to cancel this out completely. On the other hand, the receipts in advance for Year 5 were 'thrown forward' into Year 5 by treating them as creditors in the Balance Sheet of Year 4. This may sound surprising, but taken at the Balance Sheet date, if the Club had been terminated then, £30 would have had to be repaid to the members who had paid in advance.

The current subscriptions for Year 4 which have not been paid by 31 December are shown as a balance carried down on the debit side of the ledger and shown in the Balance Sheet as a current asset, in this case £46. Following the conservative accounting tradition of understating your income if there is doubt about its being received, do not include any subscription debtor which is doubtful for any reason. In this way credit is taken to the Income and Expenditure account only for true receipts.

A rather different situation arises where the Treasurer receives a Life Subscription. This will usually be a more substantial sum, and it might be thought reasonable to credit it direct to the Income and Expenditure as income received during the year and related to that year. In strict theory such a receipt shall be credited to a Life Subscription account, and each year a proportion of that sum should be credited to the Income and Expenditure account. To try to do this would be an absurdity, as the question of how long the member is going to live or remain a member of the association or society is impossible to answer. Instead it is customary to credit a Life Subscription direct to the Accumulated Fund, and it therefore bypasses the Income and Expenditure account. However, it must be admitted that this practice is not universally followed, and it is not uncommon for such subscriptions to be regarded as income for the year in which it is received. Maybe this has the merit of simplicity.

As far as possible, club members should be encouraged to pay their subscriptions by standing order or direct debit. The latter has the great advantage that in days of rapidly changing values, it enables increased subscription rates to be charged without the need for numerous alterations to existing standing orders.

Where members pay by cheque there is no special difficulty. This mainly comes in those cases where small amounts of cash are paid at regular intervals. Clubs for elderly people may have particular difficulties as it is not uncommon to have two or three scales of payment. There may be an annual subscription paid by the year, quarterly subscriptions for those unable to afford, or not prepared, to pay in one amount and the rest who pay weekly. Record-keeping for the Treasurer is very difficult in such cases. Different methods may be required to record the various categories. Loose-leaf ledger sheets may be helpful for the annual and quarterly members, while a specially ruled type of analysis book is often more practical for numerous weekly payments. With this type of book it is possible to have six months or more receipts across the pages so that receipts or outstandings are clearly shown.

From a cash control point of view, it is preferable to have a receipt book from which receipts will be issued for each subscription received. However, where small amounts are concerned and voluntary labour is used, this may not prove very practical. Instead, if entries are made each week in the Members' Subscription book, the cash column for that week should be totalled and agreed with the subscriptions recorded in the cash-book.

It is good financial practice to stamp any cheques received with the name of the club and its Bankers to guard against misappropriation.

Subscriptions give rise to a great deal of difficulty, particularly where the elderly are concerned, when the mind is not active and members may be under the impression that they have already paid. Good record-keeping will save arguments and lost tempers. Great help and advice can be obtained from your stationer if you explain the nature of your subscription problem, as there are now a number of useful devices available.

Other Income

(1) Gifts

A gift of money to a club may be small in amount or extremely large. The accounting treatment will largely depend on its purpose. Small gifts are best treated as income for the period and should be credited to the Income and Expenditure account.

Larger gifts tend to be for a specific purpose and are often of a capital nature. If a club wishes to raise money for providing expensive equipment or an extension to its premises these receipts should be credited to a separate Donations or Appeals account. To ensure that the monies are not mixed with normal club funds, it may be wiser to open a separate Bank account for the purpose. If the money is not immediately required, this account should be a Bank Deposit account or Building Society account which pays interest on the deposit. The advantage of this type of investment is that money can be withdrawn at reasonably short notice, say seven days, and there is no expense incurred. If Stock Exchange investments are purchased, there are the expenses of purchase and sale, as well as the risk of a fall in investment values.

When payments are made for the purpose for which the fund was created, these are credited to the Deposit account and debited to the Appeal account. The effect of this method of treating donations is to bypass the Income and Expenditure account.

Large donations which are received by a club and for which there is no specific purpose might well be credited to the Accumulation account direct. This has the advantage that the year-to-year figures in the Income and Expenditure account are not subject to violent fluctuations. Club members do not always realise that such gifts are not frequently received, and that by crediting such items to Income and Expenditure, any deficit in the year's activities may well be hidden.

Since there are no hard and fast rules for the treatment of donations, Club Treasurers may feel it helpful to discuss the accounting treatment of any donations they receive with their Finance Committee.

(2) Investment income

Investment income may come under two broad heads, that which is received gross and that which is subject to tax deducted at source.

The accounting entries to record the receipt of a dividend or interest are to debit the Bank account and to credit the Investment Income account. At the end of each year this is transferred to the credit of the Income and Expenditure account.

If the income received is Building Society interest, this has already had the tax paid at source, but at a special rate. No claim can be made for the repayment of this tax by a tax-exempt body. Consequently, Building Society interest is credited direct to a Building Society Interest account.

Where dividends and non-Building-Society interest are received less tax credits, the Bank account is debited and the Income account is credited with the amount of the cheque. With each receipt there should be a voucher setting out the amount of the tax credit.

To show the gross amount of the dividend or interest in the Income and Expenditure account, it will be necessary to credit the Income account and debit the Income Tax account with the amount of the tax credit.

Example

The Social Club's investments include £1800 10 per cent Debenture Stock in Clubs Ltd, interest being received half-yearly on 30 June and 31 December. The basic rate of income tax is 30 per cent.

The following are extracts from the relevant accounts recording these receipts:

Bank Account

			£	£
June	30	Debenture Interest ½ yr's interest re Clubs Ltd	90	
		Less Tax credit @ 30%	30	60
Dec.	31	Debenture Interest ½ yr's interest re Clubs Ltd	90	
		Less Tax credit @ 30%	30	60

Debenture Interest Received

			£				£
Dec.	31	T/fr Income & Expenditure A/c	180	June 3	Bank ½ yr's Interest		60
				Dec. 31	do.		60
				31	Income Tax A/c		60
			£180				£180

Income Tax Account

			£
Dec.	31	Debenture Interest received	60

It will be noticed that the income tax credits have been debited to the Income Tax account at the end of the year, but equally the Income Tax account can be debited at the time of each receipt. This is particularly necessary where a club is not liable to tax.

Clubs which have a charitable status and are registered with the Charity Commission under the Charities Act 1960 are exempt from all forms of taxation. Consequently, the debit balance on the Income Tax account represents an asset as the tax credit can be the subject of an income tax repayment claim. If, therefore, before repayment is made, an Income and Expenditure account and Balance Sheet is drawn up, the debit balance will be shown in that Balance Sheet as a debtor under the heading of 'current assets'.

Not all clubs or organisations will be in the fortunate position of being exempt from tax. In this case, at the end of the year the debit balance in the Income Tax account must be written off to the debit of the Income and Expenditure account as tax suffered.

The principle shown in the above illustration will apply equally to dividends received as well as to interest received.

Treasurers may well meet a third type of problem with interest received. This is where Bank interest and interest from some government stocks are received gross, but are still liable to income tax. Instead of the tax being deducted at source, the club will receive a separate notice of assessment for payment later. This is known as a Schedule D Case III Assessment.

Since the interest has been received gross it will be credited to the Income account direct, but when the tax assessment is paid the Bank is credited and the Income Tax account is debited. The debit balance in the Income Tax account will then be written off to the Income and Expenditure account at the end of the year as tax suffered.

It will be seen, therefore, that when a club does not have charitable status the credit side of the Income and Expenditure account will show the gross income, while the tax suffered will be shown on the debit side.

(3) Rent received

Rent received will arise from property owned by the club or association. Each rent agreement or lease will need to be inspected for the following details:

1 The amount of the rent
2 Due dates of payment
3 Whether payment is in advance or arrear
4 Whether provision is made for the lease to be renewed. If so, whether the rent is subject to negotiation or is predetermined
5 The responsibility of the tenants for repairs or improvements
6 Whether the contents of the letting shall be insured by the landlord or the tenant
7 Whether there is a reinstatement clause

Instalments of rent may be in arrear or paid in advance so that problems similar to those connected with subscriptions are incurred with the final accounts. Two main principles will help the Treasurer to get his adjustments right when preparing the Rent account. First, remember that the Income and Expenditure account is only concerned with the actual year of the accounts, so that instalments of rent which do not cover the period must be eliminated. The second principle is that only rent which will be received after the Balance Sheet date shall be included in the amount taken to the Income and Expenditure account. This follows the conservative accounting convention that you should only bring into your income items which have, or will be, received. Thus, debts which are due at the Balance Sheet date, which it is known are unlikely to be received in the following period, will not be included.

THE FITNESS CLUB

The Fitness Club owned two flats as part of its premises. Mr Fitton had the top flat at a rent of £90 per month, while Mr Jones occupied the bottom flat at £75 per month.

The Club prepares its accounts to 30 April each year. At 30 April Year 2, Mr Fitton owed the Club £90 for the month of April Year 2. Mr Jones had paid his rent for the month of May Year 3, in April Year 2.

During Year 3, £750 was received from Mr Jones in respect of the 10 months to 31 March. In the same period, Mr Fitton paid the Club £1260 covering the 14 months to 31 May Year 4. Rent of £75 due from Mr Jones for the month of April Year 3, was not received by the Club until 31 May Year 4.

The following example shows the ledger entries for rent received by the Club in regard to instalments in advance and arrear:

Rent Received Account

			£	£						£
Year 2										
April	30	Debtor – Fitton re April		90	April	30	Prepayment – Jones re May	b/d		75
Year 3					*Year 3*					
April	30	Prepayment – Fitton re May c/d		90	April	30	Bank – Jones re 10 months to 31 March			750
	30	Tfr to Income & Expenditure A/c Jones Fitton	900 1080	1980		30	Bank – Fitton re 14 months to 31 May			1260
						30	Debtor – Jones re April	c/d		75
				£2160						£2160
Year 3					*Year 3*					
April	30	Debtor – Jones re April	b/d	75	April	30	Prepayment – Fitton re May	b/d		90

It will be noticed that the effect of the adjustments is to make the transfer to the Income and Expenditure account exactly the right account for the year, i.e. Jones 12 × £75 = £900, while Fitton 12 × £90 = £1080. Subject to the remarks above regarding rent which is due at the Balance Sheet date, but not subsequently received, this transfer figure shall help the Treasurer to prove the accuracy of his adjustments which at times can be confusing.

(4) Legacies

Legacies and gifts have much in common except that the former only arises under the will of a testator who has died.

The accounting treatment is almost identical and reference may usefully be made to the section on 'gifts' earlier in this chapter. One observation may, perhaps, be made. Legacies are usually made generally with no specific purpose being given. To that extent, if it is of a material size, meaning fairly large in relation to the finance of the club, then the best way is to credit it direct to the Accumulated Fund. However, as was mentioned before, it is largely a matter of opinion whether this is the best treatment, or whether the amount should be credited to the Income and Expenditure account.

(5) Dances and socials

Most clubs hold dances or socials each year and the members put a great deal of hard work into these activities. Naturally the work is done voluntarily so that expenses are kept to a minimum. However, being human, and not receiving recognition in the form of money, people do like to receive the appreciation of their fellow members for their labours.

The presentation of accounting information in club accounts should show in the best possible manner the fullest picture of what has taken place. This is why the 'Gross' method has been used in the Frendlee Club Income and Expenditure account in the Appendix. By showing the full receipts, less the full expenses, the maximum information is given. An alternative method is simply to show the 'Net' figure. If this represents a profit on the dance it will appear on the credit side of the Income and Expenditure account, while any loss will be placed on the debit side.

The main disadvantage of the 'Net' method is that important figures such as ticket sales and expenses are hidden. These figures are of great importance to members, especially those on the Dance or Social Committee. Not only do they give a fairly good idea of the number of tickets sold, but the relationship between the income and the expenditure. People who have worked hard like to see a good sales figure for tickets sold. They also like to see that they get value for money. If the profit is too high, there will be criticism that tickets were too expensive, while, if expenditure is too high, steps may need to be taken to reduce them. Accounts provide the information on which people may base their decisions, however irrational these may be!

Two somewhat extreme examples may provide useful discussion and consideration of the problems which may arise, and also provide their solution:

Dance (a)	£	£	Dance (b)	£	£
Proceeds of sale of tickets		156			390
Less:					
Hire of band/dance equipment	60			32	
Refreshments	104			98	
Prizes, decorations	25	189		17	147
Loss		£33	Profit		£243

If the net profit/loss was shown in the Income and Expenditure, what a lot of useful information would be lost. In the case of Dance(a) there may be a good explanation for the rather poor sales figure. It may have snowed or the tickets might have proved too expensive for young people. On the other hand, the sellers may have been slack in their efforts. All sorts of explanations are therefore possible, and only with a more detailed knowledge of the Club circumstances could the real reasons be established.

Dance(b) suggests that the huge profit may have been planned for a particular purpose. The band is cheap and therefore the whole purpose of the dance may have been to raise money for Club funds or a particular project. With the figures in these accounts available, the readers will be able to interpret them in the light of their own knowledge. People often complain that they do not get this type of information, so it is most important that it is presented fully, clearly, and with an explanation if this is considered desirable.

(6) Receipts from games

Most clubs have some form of games available for their members. Frequently, these will include billiards, snooker and table tennis. A small charge is normally made to cover overheads such as electricity and repairs to the equipment. A very convenient way of collecting such a charge is to install a meter controlling the lights (which are usually essential for proper play). The rate charged should be sufficient to recover the overheads. When the meter is full, it should be emptied and the takings recorded directly into the cash-book, the money being banked as soon as possible.

Where a meter is not installed but a charge is made, then a receipt book should be used, and this would normally be made out by a helper, the top copy being handed to the player and the counterfoil being used to verify the total entered into the cash-book.

(7) Entrance fees ✳

Entrance fees may be charged in several circumstances. New members may be required to pay a fee on joining, in addition to the annual subscription. Provision should be made in the accounting records to show this clearly, and whatever system is used to deal with subscriptions can be used for this purpose also.

Entrance fees from new members will be fairly small in number, but an entrance fee in the nature of an admission charge may be made for all visitors and non-members. This may cause problems by their sheer volume. Some mechanical method may be required such as a cash register issuing a receipt. On a smaller scale, the counterfoil receipt book may be sufficient, care being taken to ensure that all monies received are duly recorded in the cash-book.

CHAPTER **7**

Bar Trading Accounts

Book-keeping

Two important requirements will largely determine the nature of the accounting records to be kept. They must provide the information required by law for VAT purposes and also give management up-to-date facts and figures on which to base their decisions.

The Treasurer may want to use the analysis cash-book for these purposes, in which case he is strongly urged to get proper professional advice from a qualified Accountant, due to the problems which can arise from VAT requirements. As an alternative, certain specialised stationers provide pre-printed layouts which reduce the book-keeping to a series of set instructions. In either case, do check with the VAT Office that the records kept comply with their requirements. (See *Value Added Tax – General Guide* Notice No. 700 issued by the Customs and Excise.)

The notes in this chapter are designed to help the Treasurer understand the prime requirements when choosing the system which meets the needs of his club, rather than providing a detailed book-keeping manual which would cover every set of circumstances.

(1) Receipts

For VAT purposes these are known as **outputs** most of which are subject to VAT at standard rate. From a management point of view, they are normally called **takings** as they arise from the sale of liquor, food, tobacco and other items in the bar.

At this stage it is important to introduce the Treasurer to two new terms, **mark up** and **gross profit**. These are the two ways of looking at the same thing – the difference between the purchase price and the selling price of a commodity. An example will help to show the difference. If goods cost, at a VAT exclusive price, 100p and a 'mark up' of 50 per cent is added, the selling price is now £1.50. However, the 'gross profit' percentage is $33\frac{1}{3}$ per cent of the selling price, i.e. the 50p added to the 100p now represents a third of the total selling price. The licensed trade defines its gross profit percentage as 'the percentage of Sale turnover, VAT exclusive', while the Customs and Excise tend to use the usual trade description 'mark up'.

It does not matter greatly which term is used, providing the significance is apparent to the reader. A point to bear in mind is that gross profit percentages are much lower than the 'mark ups'. Thus, the following are illustrative:

Mark up (%)	Converted to gross profit percentage of sales
10	9.1
45	31.0
50	33.3
60	38.0
70	41.1
90	47.4

The rates of gross profit on bar sales vary considerably. Beer is in the region of 35 per cent, wines 57 per cent, spirits 52 per cent, minerals 47 per cent and tobacco 9 per cent. Those figures will vary considerably from club to club, but they represent the sort of rates which may be expected. Consequently, it is important to know the quantities and cash values sold under each heading so that their profitability can be compared. For example, a high sale value on tobacco is not particularly profitable, whereas even a modest turnover on wines and spirits is worthwhile.

Takings need to be analysed under the following heads:

Wines ⎫
Spirits ⎪
Beers ⎬ If practical
Lager ⎪
Minerals ⎭
Tobacco
Cigarettes
Nuts, Crisps, etc.
Bar Catering
Newspapers, etc.
'Take-away' Catering

The best way of making this analysis is by using a till provided with a good cash-analysis system. Bar staff should be instructed to make the analysis of each sale as far as practical, which may be difficult in a busy bar. None the less, this information is very important from a control point of view and from a VAT angle, especially if the Customs and Excise suspect fraud over the takings.

The cash-book should not only provide full analysis under the heads discussed above, but it must also distinguish between items which bear full standard rate and those which are zero rated or exempt. Liquor, tobacco, and catering takings for consumption within Club premises will be standard rated. If catering is provided for 'take-way' service, these takings are normally zero rated, and so require careful separation from other catering takings. However, few, if any clubs, are likely to have such a facility. Sales of certain items like newspapers are exempt from VAT and require separate analysis.

An example of a cash-book ruling for receipts could be as follows:

Exempt Takings	Standard Rate Takings					Zero Rating		Total Takings	Cash	Bank
	Liquor	Tobacco	Cigarettes	Bar Catering	Others	Catering Off-sales	Others			

VAT leaflet No. 701/5/79 *Clubs and Associations – Liability to VAT* should be read by the Treasurer as it covers such matters as:

Admission charges
Amusement machines and Games of chance
Bingo
Court or Green fees
Discos
Gaming-machine takings
Match and Training fees
Prizes
Sports and other equipment sold on club premises
Lotteries
Subscriptions
Telephone coin-boxes

Failure to deal with these items correctly may result in penalties and/or additional assessments which can be disconcerting for all concerned.

(2) Payments

Cash/Bank expenditure by a club is known, for VAT purposes, as 'inputs' for goods and services.

As with receipts, proper analysis is necessary for normal accounting purposes, but in addition it is best to keep an 'invoice register' for the recording of all taxable inputs as soon as an invoice is received, whether or not it is paid immediately. The principle on which to work is to obtain a VAT invoice for all items purchased, except where this would be impractical, for example on telephone calls from a telephone coin-box. The register must be designed to give a detailed analysis of taxable purchases and expenses.

Quarterly, the register is totalled and the figures used for the VAT return to the Customs and Excise.

The layout of such a register may be under the following headings:

Date	Supplier	Invoice Number	Invoice Total	Taxable Inputs							Exempt Inputs	VAT	Cash-book Ref.
				Repairs	Beers	Wines & Spirits	Minerals	Tobacco	Food Purchases				

Note – The cash-book reference column is inserted so that the date of payment of each item can be inserted.

(3) VAT account

Once per quarter, which does not necessarily mean calendar quarters, the Treasurer must prepare a VAT return for submission to the Customs and Excise. The method used is to prepare a VAT account showing the total VAT due on takings, less the VAT suffered on expenditure. Normally there will be an excess of 'outputs' over 'inputs', in which case the Treasurer will send a cheque to the Customs and Excise for this sum with the return. In the rare cases where 'inputs' exceed 'outputs', a cheque will be received from Customs and Excise after submission of the return.

Provision is made on the return for under or over declarations in respect of VAT due and also for any under or over payments due.

(4) Bar wages

One or more staff will be employed to run the bar and a proper wages book should be used. This should show the calculation of the gross wage, deductions for National Insurance and PAYE, together with the employer's contribution for National Insurance and pension. A helpful leaflet is published by the Inland Revenue entitled *The Employers Guide – PAYE*.

Do not forget that each employee requires a contract of employment under the Employment Protection (Consolidation) Act 1978.

(5) Bar stock records

The basis of any successful bar is a good stock control system. So far, the analysis of sales and purchases has been described in detail. Now it is necessary to look at the stock records themselves. Today, probably the best system for a club is to use a loose-leaf stock ledger containing overlapping ledger sheets held in a convenient sized loose-leaf file. The object of the overlapping ledger sheets is to allow the leading edge of each sheet to be visible so that the details of the stock on that sheet can be quickly identified. A separate ledger sheet should be opened for each type of stock. A typical ruling will be as follows:

	Date	Ref. No.	IN	OUT	BAL.	Price	Value	Date Ordered	Ref. No.
				Stock Record Card					
1									
2									
3									
4									
5									
6									
7									

Stock – MAX.   MIN.
Date stock checked
DESCRIPTION

Each day a stock requisition form should be completed by the barman showing his requirements for restocking the bar. This enables the individual stock record sheets just described to be completed in respect of the items from the stores.

Stock record cards are entered up direct from supplies invoices, hence the reference number column is important. Stock records are mainly concerned with physical quantities, but the purchase price of each stock delivery should be recorded, although the value column will normally be left blank. At the end of the financial year, or if required for interim stock-taking, the value column can be completed to assist with the stock-taking process.

Control

At first sight running a bar may appear to be a fairly simple matter; after all it is just a question of employing a barman, deciding on the prices to be charged, and then sitting back waiting for the profits, if any.

The reader may be very surprised to even contemplate a bar making a loss, but unfortunately managing a bar is quite a complex operation which must be approached on proper management principles, otherwise substantial losses may be incurred very quickly without anyone even suspecting the possibility.

First, a Bar Committee needs to be formed to act as a Management Committee on behalf of the members, and to assist the Treasurer who should be a full member of the Committee. The task of the Committee will be to have full charge of the operation of the bar, controlling its day-to-day detailed workings. The actual details will depend completely on the nature of the club, its members, and the extent to which the bar is operated. Thus, only broad principles can be considered in this chapter.

Perhaps it would be helpful to point out the nature of the problems that need to be tackled so that the reader will have a better understanding of the control techniques which will be considered.

Liquor and tobacco are items of fairly high value and are readily marketable. They are also capable of being consumed on club premises by staff or members, without payment. Liquor, in particular, can be subject to a great deal of manipulation. For example, the number of 'tots' from a bottle may be increased by one or two, although there are 'acceptable' figures. Thus, 31 are obtainable from a 26 oz. bottle, or 46 from a 40 oz. bottle. There is also the question of 'ullage', breakages, blowings and rejections. Unless there are clearly-defined methods of dealing with these items the system will be wide open to abuse. To add to these problems there are also the risks of suppression of takings and the misappropriation of cash.

In some ways this section of the chapter may be more important than the rest, because even if records are well kept, unless they are used intelligently, their value will be wasted.

To understand the 'control system', it must be appreciated that there are two separate but related aspects. First, there is the control of physical items – the actual quantities of stock involved and, second, their cash values.

For the purpose of this chapter, it is assumed that the stock in the bar is separate from the stock in the store, and that daily stock requisitions or 'transfers' forms are completed showing the physical quantities transferred from the stores to the bar.

At a given point, the stocks in both the bar and the stores should be taken. The store stocks must completely agree with the stock record sheets. Remember that we are concerned here with quantities, not values.

From this starting point, each supplier's invoice should be fully recorded in the stock ledger sheets in respect of the quantities of purchases taken into stock, the balance columns being completed each time. From a control point of view, it is very desirable that the stock ledger should be written up by a person who is not in any way concerned with the running of the bar. This is to avoid any risk of manipulation of the control system. It forms a part of what is called in management terms the 'system of internal check'. Likewise, the daily stock requisitions completed by the barman are entered, and the requisitions filed away and retained.

At frequent intervals, not less than monthly, the store stock should be physically taken and reconciled with the stock record cards. Stock-taking can be done by the Bar Committee or some delegated members. Any differences between the physical count and the stock records requires careful investigation. Suppliers' invoices should be checked against the stock record sheets concerned, the balances also being checked. Requisitions are also checked from those on the file, and if the difference is not due to inaccurate record-keeping, the question of breakages, spillage, etc. needs to be considered carefully. At the same time, it is essential to consider who has access to the stock-room. In theory, the barman should be excluded entirely, and the stock taken into store and checked by another person. It may be possible for members of the Committee to undertake the task, as it is very important that the barman cannot influence this part of the stock. This is the ideal position as it reduces the risk of fraud considerably, and will therefore be assumed to be the system used by most clubs. The reader will note that it enables a tight control to be kept on the store stock, providing the problems of wastage, spillage and leakages are dealt with. Advice is always available from suppliers on the accepted quantities for these purposes.

This leaves the problem of the control of the bar. Bar stock should be checked frequently, usually at the same time as the store stocks, so that there is no question of the switching of stocks to make up for any deficiencies in the others. Those doing the checking of bar stocks should be on the look-out for unauthorised brands, as bar stewards have been known to substitute their own cheaper brands and pocket the difference.

Bar consumption record

If the daily stock requisition prepared by the barman is provided with a cash column as well as with quantities columns, it is possible to provide a much tighter management control system.

The author has seen a successful system in operation based on this method. The club 'loaned' the Bar Steward a sufficient sum of money to fund the running of the bar. He was then 'bonded' for this amount, the club taking out an insurance policy for fidelity guarantee. Thus, if the Bar Steward absconded with the takings, the loss could be claimed under the insurance policy.

Each day the Steward completed his stock requisition for restocking the bar, the requisition showing both quantities and their value at selling price. This was then charged to him personally, and he paid the Treasurer out of the monies loaned to him so that the 'profit' was made at this stage and not when the sales were made to the members in the bar. However, under this system, it was necessary to make the normal allowances for wastage, leakages, returns, etc.

By preparing separate summaries of the stock movements in the store and in the bar, it is possible to check on the financial performance of the bar and to isolate the various factors which make that up. These summaries are memorandum by nature and are often known as bar consumption records, and can be prepared in analysis books.

(a) Store stock

The stock quantity columns will be a summary of the stock movements shown on the stock card of an item in the stock ledger. The cost price of the item can also be taken from the stock card.

STORE STOCK

Period Covered

Stock Item	Opening Stock	Pur-chases	Trans-fers to Bar	Allow-ances, etc.	Clos-ing Stock	Cost Price of Stock Item	Value at Cost Price of Transfers to Bar	Bar Selling Price of Stock Item	Sale Value of Trans-fers to Bar	Gross Profit or Mark-up

Care should be taken to ensure that the transfers to the bar are charged at the prices displayed in the bar, and the column marked 'Sale value of transfers to bar' should be totalled at the end of the summary. This is a valuable control figure. It should be capable of reconciliation with the total of all the requisitions made by the barman during the period, and thus equal to the total cash paid by him to the Treasurer.

If the 'Value at cost price of transfers to bar' column is completed, this can be deducted from the 'Sale value of transfers to bar' column to give the amount of the gross profit or mark-up.

From a management point of view, this summary can be of considerable value. It enables the reader to see in a very convenient form the performance of each stock item. Not only is the quantitative stock position easy to see, but the financial performance as well. Unprofitable lines need to be identified quickly, and either eliminated or action taken to improve their performance. Some items, like tobacco, give impressive figures of turnover but yield a low rate of profit.

Treasurers should be aware that the Inspector of Taxes and the VAT officers will use this system of working out what gross profit or mark-up should have been made on each line sold in the bar, and if the takings disclosed are less, estimated assessments are likely to be issued. It is for the club to prove, at its own expense, to the contrary. Bar Committees must therefore clearly establish a selling policy which is understood by members, bar staff and outsiders such as tax and VAT officials.

(b) Bar stock

The purpose of this summary is to act as a check on the cash takings recorded by the barman, and it is based on similar principles to the store stock control above.

BAR STOCK

Period Covered

Stock Item	Opening Stock	Trans- fers from Stores	Allow- ances, etc.	Clos- ing Stock	Goods Sold	Bar Selling Price of Stock Item	Value of Opening Stock	Value of Transfer from Store	Value of Closing Stock	Value of Goods Sold

The quantity of the opening stock in the bar and its value at selling price will be known from the previous period. Similarly, the quantities transferred from the store during the period under review can be picked up from the store stock summary together with their values. By physically taking the closing stock, the quantities of stock sold can be computed. Both should be calculated at selling price. After allowing for any losses, returns etc., the following calculation can be made:

          £

Value of Opening Stock
Add Transfers from Store   _____

Less Value of Closing Stock _____
∴ Value of Goods Sold   ======

It is this 'Value of goods sold' which should reconcile with the recorded takings. If there is any material difference, all ledger entries and summaries will need to be checked to see that there are no clerical errors causing the difference. A full investigation should then be carried out, and it may also be necessary to suspend the barman until the position has been clarified.

The reader may feel at this point that the circumstances of his particular club do not permit the luxury of the detailed system above. Instead, a simpler system is needed, but it must be clearly understood that the risks involved must also be the greater.

The main difference in a simpler system will normally be that the Steward is responsible for the complete handling of the stocks, both bar and store, so that the risk of manipulation is much greater. As far as possible, the procedure described above should be followed, but the physical checking of the bar and store stocks should be much more frequent, say roughly once a week. These checks should be at irregular times so that if fraud is being perpetrated, it will be made more difficult as the Steward will not be sure when his stock and records are going to be checked.

One point to look for is any pattern emerging in differences which are discovered. It may show that the Steward is consuming a particular item such as brandy or cigarettes, and his personal habits may give a clue to the reason for the differences. One golden rule is helpful for the Committee to observe. The Steward and bar staff should have included in their contracts of employment conditions whereby, in the event of any difference which is suspicious or material, they can be sacked immediately or suspended on full pay until the problem has been investigated and solved. Any delay in removing the staff from their duties can only be detrimental to the club.

Audit Points

The functions of the Honorary Auditor in relation to bar trading are threefold:

1 To check the accuracy of the book-keeping and other records.
2 To verify the physical stocks and reconcile them with the stock records.
3 To ensure that the system of controls operates.

As has been said earlier in this chapter, bar stocks are items of reasonably high value and are by their nature easily misappropriated in a number of ways. The Auditor must be alive to these various possibilities when carrying out his audits as he is the person entrusted with the task of protecting the club and members against fraud. However, one must say quite clearly, this is not the purpose of the audit, but rather a by-product.

(1) Cash receipts

Cash receipts require special attention. The cash-book entries should be vouched with the till receipts, care being taken to ensure that the dates and totals are entered correctly. The figures extended into the analysis columns must likewise be carefully checked, as if the analysis is done incorrectly a number of errors could follow. For example, if tobacco receipts are shown as wines or spirits, calculation of the gross profit percentage would give very misleading results. VAT assessments may be wrongly based and the Inspector of Taxes may also start investigations if the gross profit percentages look out of the general trend for a particular item.

Monies paid into the Bank should be verified by reference to the pay-in slips. Check that the detailed make-up of banking shown by the slips is correctly and fully recorded in the cash-book. If the total is the same in each place, but the detail is different, the fraud of *teeming and lading* may be taking place. This is best described as 'borrowing from Peter to pay Paul'. If it is suspected, make a detailed examination of the cash-book with pay-in slips and any counterfoil receipt books. If necessary ask a qualified Accountant to advise you, or the police.

(2) Cash payments

Cash payments will be vouched in the manner described in Chapter 9. If a bar is operated, the main points to look for are the analysis of payments and their treatment for VAT purposes.

(3) VAT records

VAT records also form part of the Auditor's duties. The VAT register should be vouched with the files of invoices which should be kept in the same sequence as the register. Ensure that the VAT analysis is correct. At the end of each quarter, if returns are done on this basis, check the totals from the register to the returns. Payments to the Customs and Excise will be vouched by reference to their receipts.

(4) Stock and stock records

Physical verification of bar and store stocks is very important and should be carried out, if possible, in the presence of members of the Bar Committee delegated to undertake this task.

Stock records should be reconciled with the stock physically checked. This means that the receipts and issues of stock should be allowed for when adjusting for the time-lag between taking the stock and any entries to be made on the stock record cards.

Ensure that stocks are valued at cost price, not selling price.

If there are any old stocks which are unsaleable or which have deteriorated, they should be written off completely or reduced in value to 'net realisable value'. (This is sale price less costs of selling, if any.)

Check the system of recording stock receipts on to the stock record cards. This is done from the suppliers' invoices and is concerned with the physical quantities, but the correct purchase prices should be noted on the cards.

Select a number of daily requisitions and check these to the stock cards. Ensure that the prices at which the goods are issued to the bar are at selling price. Verify by reference to the lists shown publicly in the bar. Enquire into the system of allowances for wastage, returns, breakages, etc. Ensure that the system is being adhered to.

Enquire into the frequency of the checking of stocks by Bar Committee members.

They should sign a register each time that this is done, giving a note of any problems, to be followed by a note of the action taken and its outcome.

Consider whether the stock maximum and minimum figures are reasonable. If considered excessive, discuss with the Committee.

Purchases of bar stocks should be done on an official order-form and signed by at least two members of the Committee appointed for the purpose.

When examining the purchase invoices, check that the invoices are correctly addressed to the club, that the purchase is one that is reasonable having regard to the nature of the club, and that the place of delivery is the club itself, not to someone's private address.

(5) Bar consumption records

The nature of this has already been explained, and the entries and calculations should be checked from the basic records. This book is important as it acts as a control on the whole system. The actual takings should be reconciled with the value of stock issued to the bar.

CHAPTER **8**

Value Added Tax

It would be inappropriate in a book of this nature to attempt to describe the workings of the VAT system. There are a number of books on the market which are devoted to the topic, and which endeavour to guide their readers through the highly technical legislation. In addition to these books, the Customs and Excise publish a number of leaflets giving up-to-date information on a variety of topics. These leaflets highlight two important points. The first is the problem of keeping up to date. Even before publication, many tax books are out of date due to the time-lag between the writing and final publication. Updated leaflets largely overcome this problem. They also assist with the second problem. With the great variety of situations arising with VAT, no textbook can hope to deal with all its aspects. Specialised information can thus be provided easily on individual topics or for particular trades.

Club Treasurers should be aware that VAT is, in some ways, far more complex in its application than the other traditional forms of taxation such as income and capital gains taxation. Its ramifications are often felt in the most unlikely places. Common sense is not a reliable guide, and may indeed lead a Treasurer into very serious trouble. As the person responsible for a club's finances, he should obtain a copy of the leaflet *Should I be registered for VAT* and study it carefully.

At the same time, it would be convenient to obtain copies of the following:

Value Added Tax – General Guide No. 700
*   – Scope & Charge No. 701*
*   – Clubs & Associations Liability to Tax No. 701/5/79*
*   – Charities No. 701/1/79*
*   – on gaming-machine takings No. 9/78/VAH*
*   – re Bar Sales – 'Scheme A' – Special Schemes for Retailers No. 727*

A quick glance through these publications will probably convince the average Treasurer that he 'doesn't want to know'. However, as a responsible official of the club he may be liable to penalties if the law on VAT is not complied with. To protect himself and the club, good professional advice should be obtained to ensure that if VAT legislation does apply to the club, proper records are kept to enable correct VAT returns to be submitted. It must be stressed that this is really no job for the amateur, however willing.

72

Further advice is available at VAT offices, and VAT officers will be especially pleased to guide Treasurers in ensuring that club records are suitable for the task.

For Treasurers of charitable clubs there is a further word of warning. By virtue of their charitable status, such clubs will be exempt from other forms of taxation, but this does not necessarily mean exemption from VAT. The leaflet on 'Charities' mentioned above gives a very valuable outline of the problem. After reading this and other leaflets, one begins to appreciate the all-pervading nature of the tax which can so easily have disastrous ramifications which are not realised until it is too late.

At this stage a word may not be out of place regarding the books of account required to provide the information required by VAT legislation. These books must also provide the normal financial information for accounting purposes and, in many cases, as a basis for taxation. Such records need to be sufficiently detailed to record the information fully but, at the same time, as simply as possible to enable Treasurers who are not really versed in book-keeping to maintain them accurately.

A useful answer to this problem is provided by certain stationers who supply specially-designed account books. These books normally provide separate pages for each week's transactions, with yearly summaries at the back. These in turn lead to draft final accounts which are merely completed with the figures from the summaries. Such books also have various methods for 'proving' the accuracy of the book-keeping week by week. If well kept these are very helpful, but if kept by a 'Muddler' of a Treasurer they can prove to be an extremely expensive investment in time, effort and consequences.

The rulings of these books also provide full analysis of takings and expenditure to comply with VAT regulations. Clubs may provide goods and services for members and, depending on the nature of these items, analysis will be needed under the headings of standard rating, zero rating and exempt takings. Expenditure, or 'inputs' as they are usually called in VAT terminology, must be similarly recorded.

Reference should be made to Chapter 7 Bar Trading Accounts where this topic is dealt with in more detail.

CHAPTER **9**

Help for the Auditor

The Choice of Auditor

As with other organisations, there is an increasing trend towards 'openness' in the running of clubs and associations. In the past, members have mainly been content to leave this to officials such as the President/Chairman and Secretary, and to members of the Committee. For practical reasons, the day-to-day control of affairs must be vested in those officials, of whom the Treasurer is one. A great deal of hard work is done voluntarily by these 'unsung heroes' who do not always receive the credit for their efforts. Often, members who do not bother to take much active part in the running of their organisation complain that they do not know what is going on and that the organisation is being run by a 'clique'. One way of removing this type of complaint is by regularly producing some type of club bulletin or news-letter. This will include information on club events, details of club officials, and from time to time financial information.

Much has been said in the earlier part of this book about the need for the members to decide the type of financial information that they require, and the best format for its presentation. Having made their decision, the next job is to ensure that the information presented to the members is accurate and reliable and this is where the Treasurer and the Auditor come in. They are complementary and their work will to some extent overlap.

The job of the Treasurer is twofold. First, he is responsible for the day-to-day record-keeping of the financial affairs of the organisation, by keeping proper books of account. Second, at the end of the financial year, he should acquire sufficient skill to produce a set of final accounts of the type discussed in the early chapters of this book. At this stage the Auditor takes over, it not being his task to prepare the accounts. His job is to carefully examine the year's transactions leading up to the final accounts, and to see that they have been properly incurred and recorded. Then he examines the final accounts to ensure that they show a 'true and fair view' of the financial position of the organisation at the end of the financial year. Last, he reports to the members of the organisation by attaching his report to the final accounts which are, in due course, circulated to members and other interested persons.

It may be felt that the job of Auditor is unnecessary as the Treasurer is trusted completely. This trust, one hopes, will be fully justified in every case, and it is no reflection on the ability or integrity of any Treasurer that he should be asked to submit his work to the scrutiny of an Auditor; being human he will make mistakes from time to time. The office of Auditor goes back at least several thousand years to Roman times when the accounts were 'heard' by the Auditors. Over the centuries, it was regarded as an office of honour as it was given to people who were regarded as being of high integrity. However, during the latter part of the nineteenth century, the complexity of accounting requirements grew to an extent that required the services of qualified Accountants and Auditors. This was the reason for the rise of the accounting profession in the 1870s and 1880s.

While it is best to employ a professionally qualified Auditor and, indeed, a legal requirement for clubs subject to the Companies Acts 1948 to 1980, most clubs will appoint an Honorary Auditor who is not a qualified Accountant, but who nevertheless displays a number of special qualities. In some ways, the most important are integrity and independence, although business experience and familiarity with money matters are also useful attributes. Integrity is a quality which those who appoint him must judge, while independence must be seen to be the case. 'Independence' implies that there is no family or emotional relationship with the Treasurer and no financial involvement, directly or indirectly. As was said by Lord Justice Lindley in re London & General Bank No. 2 (1895), 'An Auditor must be honest, that is, he must not certify what he does not believe to be true, and he must take reasonable care and skill before he believes that what he certifies is true.'

Other qualities include the need for accuracy and diligence, as he is there to detect the mistakes or fraud of others. Courage of conviction is frequently needed if there is a genuine query or an item which is largely a matter of opinion. From time to time, pressure may be brought on the Auditor to dissuade him from a course of action which he feels should be taken. This is when 'independence' is so important. It may be that certain expenditure is 'dubious' or 'sensitive' in that it is not strictly in accordance with the club policy or authority, or is made for personal gain. Life can become 'uncomfortable' for the Auditor, and he will have to be prepared to face this.

As for the duties of an Auditor, perhaps this can be shown by another judicial extract, this time from another famous case re Kingston Cotton Mill Co. (No. 2) 1896. 'It is the duty of an Auditor to bring to bear on the work he has to perform, that skill, care and caution which a reasonably competent, careful and cautious Auditor would use. What is reasonable skill, care and caution must depend on the particular circumstances of each case. . . . If there is anything calculated to excite suspicion, he should probe it to the bottom, but in the absence of anything of that kind he is only bound to be reasonably cautious and careful. . . . The duties of the Auditor must not be rendered too onerous.'

It is worth remembering that these cases are old, and that the remarks were applied to professional Auditors. None the less, they do give a very good indication of what the public may expect of a club Auditor, be he qualified or not.

The Treasurer's Contribution

The Treasurer can contribute a great deal to the efficient running of the financial affairs of the organisation if he observes some basic rules of organisation. The following observations may be of assistance:

(1) During the year

The Bank statements, cheque books and pay-in books should be kept in a separate wallet file so that they can easily be handled. Bank statements should be sent automatically by the Bank at regular intervals. The frequency should be sufficient to enable regular Bank reconciliation to be done, generally monthly.

With regard to cheque payments, there should be a supporting bill, invoice or receipt for each cash-book entry. Starting at the beginning of the year, each such item is given a number, and vouchers should be filed away in sequence in a proper correspondence or hard-backed file.

Any documentary information on receipts should be similarly treated. Letters and copy invoices sent out by the Treasurer will all go on the file. When members pay a subscription, a proper receipt book should be used. The cash-book entry will record the member's name, amount and the receipt number so that there is a cross-reference available.

Copies of all letters sent out should be taken and filed in any convenient sequence. For small clubs, date sequence is sufficient, but for bigger clubs or for important items, separate correspondence files will be needed. Inward correspondence will similarly be dealt with.

(2) At the end of the year

When the Treasurer has drafted up the final accounts, he should put the books and papers ready for the Auditor. Few things give rise to more frustration than when an Auditor is presented with a jumble of papers and told 'I am sorry about this, but I got in such a muddle'. It is a reflection on the competence of the Treasurer, however conscientious he may be.

The following is a check-list which might be of help:

1 Check that the Bank statements are consecutive and that they cover the last day of the prior period as well as the last day of the current period.
2 Ensure that Bank statements or passbooks are available for all Bank accounts, including Deposit accounts and Investment accounts.

3 Check that the cash-book is added, balances carried down and all entries posted to the ledger. Ledger accounts should be added and entries ruled off where necessary.
4 Prepare a final Bank reconciliation.
5 Prepare a schedule of outstanding amounts at the Balance Sheet date together with details of stock and prepayments.
6 Prepare schedules of club assets including furniture, equipment and investments.
7 Ensure that share certificates, passbooks or other documents of title are available for inspection by the Auditor.
8 Put the files of Bank statements, cheque books and pay-in books together with files of receipts and correspondence ready for the Auditor.
9 Prepare any extracts from the minutes which may concern the Auditor.
10 Make the minute book available for inspection.
11 Put all receipt books – used, current and unused – ready for inspection.
12 Make a note of the cash balance at the date of the final accounts. (Vouchers and cash must be inspected from that date up to the time the cash balance is verified by the Auditor, so they should be kept to hand.)
13 Prepare and certify a schedule of bar stock, if any. (This should be signed by at least two people who have taken part in the stock-taking.)
14 Prepare typed copy of final accounts with supporting schedules of information regarding any important items. Ensure that it contains comparative figures for the previous year.
15 Attach a copy of the previous accounts to this year's final accounts.
16 Prepare draft of any report to be submitted to members.
17 Check that the club insurance policies are up to date and available for inspection.

The Audit Programme

The following programme will cover the needs of the average club or association. If further help is needed, professional assistance should be obtained. Textbooks are also a valuable source of information.

(1) Cash-book – general

1 Cast and cross cast all columns of the cash-book.
2 Check all postings to the ledger.
3 Check the cash-book with the Bank statements and reconcile the balances at two dates during the year, and at the year end.
4 Count any cash balances remaining in the hands of the Treasurer. Do so in his presence. All receipts and payments of cash from the Balance Sheet date up to the date of counting must be examined.

5 Obtain the club's authority for their Bank to supply, direct to the Auditor, a certificate of the balances on all accounts in the name of the club at the Balance Sheet date.

The certificate should also give details of any accounts closed during the year, and of any charges over the assets of the club. If there are any such charges, the nature of the assets charged will be indicated.

6 All payments should be vouched with a supporting receipt, invoice, bill or statement. If any are missing, copies should be requested. The Treasurer should be advised to ensure that documentary evidence is available for each transaction.

Not only will the date, name of payee and the amount be checked, but the voucher itself should bear evidence that it has been passed for payment. The minutes of the Committee may need to be inspected to ensure that authority was given for payment of the more important items.

Consider whether the nature of the transaction is appropriate to the club. Check to see the address to which goods or services were supplied. Query if there is any doubt. Do not be put off with glib explanations. Where necessary, ask for further supporting evidence such as correspondence.

7 Receipts should in general be verified as in 6 above. See below for particular items.

(2) The ledger

1 Check all additions.
2 Using the schedules of debtors, creditors and prepayments, verify the ledger entries in respect of these.
3 Check all inter-ledger transfers ensuring that there is a proper reason for them.
4 Check postings from petty-cash book.
5 Check entries from ledger accounts into Income and Expenditure account and Balance Sheet.
6 Agree details of supporting schedules.

(3) Petty cash

1 Count the cash balance in the presence of the Treasurer.
2 Vouch all payments with supporting vouchers up to the date the balance is counted, checking analysis of each item.
3 Check postings to petty-cash book from main cash-book.
4 Cast and cross cast petty-cash book for whole period.
5 Check postings to ledger or any summary.

(4) Specific items – receipts

1 Vouch cash-book receipts with receipt book counterfoils, ensuring that the former records the date, payer's name, amount and receipt number.
2 Check postings from cash-book into membership register and into the Subscriptions Received account in the ledger.
3 At the year end ensure that only subscriptions for the year covered by the Income and Expenditure account are included in that account. Examine the Subscriptions account in the ledger for this purpose.
4 Unpaid subscriptions at the Balance Sheet date should only be included as outstanding debtors if subsequently received.

(a) Gifts received

These should be vouched by reference to correspondence and receipt book. The minute book may include reference to gifts and whether any conditions are imposed by their donors.

Consider whether they should be credited to the Income and Expenditure account or the Accumulated Fund.

(b) Legacies

The treatment is similar to that for gifts received. Correspondence with the executors or their solicitors should give full details, and state whether or not the legacy is given for a particular purpose. The nature of its purpose could affect the treatment in the final accounts. (See notes on this topic – page 57.)

(c) Interest received

1 Vouch each receipt in the cash-book with the tax credit voucher.
2 Check postings from cash-book to Interest Received account.
3 Ensure that all instalments of interest due have been received. If interest is outstanding at the Balance Sheet date, treat as a debtor, but only if it is subsequently received.
4 If interest has been received less tax credits, check amount of credits with the credit vouchers from Income Tax account to Interest Received account.
5 Where interest is received gross, as in the case of Bank deposit interest, ensure that proper provision is made for the subsequent Schedule D Case III income tax assessment to be raised by the Inland Revenue in due course. This should be included under current liabilities in the Balance Sheet.

(d) Rents received

1 The rent books or lease should be inspected to determine the due dates of payment, the amount and whether payments are in advance or arrear.
2 Check all rents due have been received. Vouch prepayments and/or arrears.

3 Inspect the lease for details of responsibility for internal and external repairs, and whether there is a dilapidations clause requiring the occupant to restore the premises to its original condition on the expiration of the lease. Consider whether proper provision has been made for repairs.

4 Inspect the Club's insurance policy to ensure that full insurance cover is in force to cover fire risk on the building and, where necessary, the contents. Other risks, such as landlord's liability to the tenant and third parties, burglary etc. should be covered. Contact the insurance company for their advice, if necessary.

5 If rent is in arrears, inspect correspondence with solicitors, tenants, etc. Request club to confirm in writing the steps being taken to recover the outstanding instalments.

(e) Dividends received

Dividends received are usually subject to a tax credit, meaning that only the net sum is received. Each dividend should be vouched by reference to the tax credit voucher. Reference should be made to the heading above of 'Interest received' for audit details.

If the club or organisation enjoys charitable status, check that repayment claims have been made for the income-tax credits which accompany any instalment of interest or payment of dividend, subject to income tax. If a claim is outstanding at the Balance Sheet date, an accurate estimate of the amount due for repayment should be made and included under the current assets as a debtor.

(f) Fruit machine

A number of machines are available for club use, both of a true gaming nature and for gambling. Some of these require a certain amount of money to be left within the machine and this should be determined by a club official.

As a safeguard, the keys to these machines should not be available to the Treasurer or anyone concerned with counting cash. It is recommended that they be left in a safe or cupboard with at least two locks so that two or more people are aware of when the keys are in use.

Two persons should be present when the machines are unlocked and the cash removed. As a further precaution, a third person should count the cash left in the machines, as well as that removed. This should be done in the presence of the other two. The cash should be entered into the pay-in book and banked as soon as possible.

For the benefit of members, Inland Revenue and Customs and Excise, a record should be kept of the date the machines are emptied, the amount left in the machines and the amount removed and banked. This should be signed by the parties to the transaction.

Report to the members and the committee any weaknesses in the system of dealing with cash from machines.

(g) Receipts from games

Most clubs have games available for members for which a charge is made. The most common will be billiards, snooker and table tennis.

The simplest system for making a charge is to use a slot meter which operates the lighting system. The charge should be sufficient to cover overheads. A record should be made of the date the meter is emptied, the amount collected and the person responsible. This should be vouched to the cash-book.

If no meter is employed, the best alternative method is to use a receipt book, the top copy being given to players on payment of fees. The counterfoil receipts would be vouched to the cash-book. Spoiled receipts should be retained in the receipt book to show that they have not been fraudulently used.

Some clubs retain a small cash-book and separate cash box for games receipts. This should be cast and the amounts of cash transferred to the main cash-book, verified.

If the amounts involved are significant, thought should be given to installing an improved system.

(h) Dances and socials

The majority of club dances and socials make a profit and so are included under the receipts section of the chapter.

The correct accounting treatment for dances and socials was considered on page 58.

Request the accounts of the Dance or Social committee who usually run these affairs, vouch with any supporting vouchers and count the balance of Cash in Hand in the presence of the holder. Consider club policy on dances and socials. Ensure that the Dance/Social accounts are correctly reflected in the final accounts.

(i) Bar receipts

Reference should be made to Chapter 7 Bar Trading Accounts.

(j) Sales of refreshments

1 Verify payments with invoices, bills or receipts.
2 Payments should be made by cheque where possible, but some will have to be made by cash. A petty-cash imprest system should be used for this purpose.
    The imprest system should be verified as mentioned under 'Petty cash' earlier in the chapter.
3 Stocks of food should be taken at the Balance Sheet date and certified by the person responsible for the running of the refreshment counter.
4 Daily takings should, where possible, be recorded on a till with a paper tape. These tapes should be retained and the totals checked against the cash-book. Select, say, three months tapes at intervals during the year to check with the cash-book.
5 Note the amount of cash retained in the till for change.

6 Check the rate of gross profit percentage compared with previous years. If materially different, enquire into the reasons for the change.

If the rate of gross profit is not reasonable, bearing in mind that prices charged may be low when compared with prices outside, then such a low rate may indicate fraud or faulty accounting.

Enquire into club policy about the sale of refreshments. If necessary, discuss the matter with the Catering Committee.

(5) Specific items – payments

(a) Wages and salaries

Depending on the number of employees, the Auditor should select two or three periods during the year, preferably of one month each, and should apply the following procedure:

1 Inspect the contracts of employment for all employees.
2 Confirm that the employer holds a tax deduction card for each employee, together with a notice of coding. Check that the correct code number was applied at the date of each monthly period selected for testing.
3 Vouch gross wages by reference to contracts of employment. Ensure that overtime payments are authorised.
4 Check individual deductions for National Insurance and Superannuation. Check totals deducted to appropriate ledger accounts.
5 Down cast and cross cast all columns of wages book.
6 Check monthly remittance to H.M. Collector of Taxes of PAYE, National Insurance and Superannuation contributions.
7 Verify employer's contribution to National Insurance and Superannuation. Check postings for these accounts to the Wages or Salaries accounts.
8 If casual labour or part-time assistance is used, check that the name and address of the payee is available, and that a signature is obtained for each payment.

If payments exceed the non-taxable limit, check that tax has been deducted in accordance with the prevailing PAYE system. Reference should be made to the Employers Guide issued by the Inland Revenue.
9 Holiday pay should be verified by reference to the contracts of employment. Test a certain proportion of the calculation of amounts paid to employees in respect of holiday pay.
10 Enquire into the club's policy regarding sickness pay.

If it is a policy to make up the difference between sickness benefit from the Department of Health and Social Security and normal wages, check that proper evidence of sickness is obtained by the club. Medical certificates should be required after the normal three-day period of illness.

Payments of benefit can be verified by the claimant producing to the club the remittance slip giving details of benefit payments.

(b) Rent paid

1 Inspect the rent book or lease, check the amount payable, dates of payment and whether the rent is payable in advance or arrear.
2 Verify Rent account, vouch each payment with a receipt or entry in rent book.
3 Treat as a provision any instalment of rent due at the Balance Sheet date, and include as a Creditor under current liabilities.
4 Note any terms in the lease regarding repairs. Check that proper provision is made in the accounts for any actual or potential liabilities in this respect. Tenants are usually responsible for decorations while landlords are liable for structural repairs.
5 Inspect the insurance policy to ensure that full cover is in force for fire and other risks, particularly theft, damage and liability to third parties. Tenants normally insure the contents but not the building.

Index-linked policies are strongly advised.

(c) Rates

These are easily verified by reference to the rating demand, but particular attention must be paid to the question of whether any part of the rates are in advance or arrear. Much depends on the Balance Sheet date in relation to the date of payment.

Check the calculations and the amounts on to the schedules of outstandings and prepayments.

(d) Water rate

These follow similar principles to the rating verification.

(e) Heat and light

1 Vouch payments by reference to suppliers' invoices.
2 Estimate consumption from last quarterly reading (re gas and electricity), up to the date of the Balance Sheet. Treat as an outstanding expense.
3 Calculate stocks of fuel (coal and oil) at the date of the Balance Sheet. Deduct from total heating and lighting expenses for the year, showing the net expense in the Income and Expenditure account, while the stocks appear under the current assets in the Balance Sheet.

(f) Bar expenses

See Chapter 7 Bar Trading Accounts for details.

(g) Depreciation

1 Obtain a schedule of the club's fixed assets.

2 Consider whether the rate of depreciation is sufficient for each asset, and whether the method of computation is appropriate.

The method used in the Frendlee Club example is known as the fixed percentage or reducing instalment method. The depreciation is calculated by reference to a chosen rate calculated on the written-down figure brought forward from last year.

In contrast the straight line, or equal instalment, method may be preferred. The cost of the asset is divided by the number of years it is expected to be used. The product is the annual rate of depreciation used each year to write the asset off completely, e.g.

Car – cost £4000
Expected use in business – 5 years

$$\frac{£4000}{5} = £800 \text{ p.a. depreciation}$$

In times of inflation the straight line method has much to recommend it.

(h) Insurance

1 Verify payments with the annual renewal notices.

2 Check that the cover is 'comprehensive', meaning that the policies cover all reasonable risks.

3 Check that the amounts insured are sufficient having regard to inflation. Index-linked policies provide the best protection.

4 Check the calculation of the prepayments at the date of the Balance Sheet ensuring that it is correctly shown in the final accounts.

Working Papers

A good set of working papers is essential for the Auditor to do his job properly. These papers should explain in detail the make-up of the figures in the final accounts and give background information to support them. In addition, they should provide a full record of all the work undertaken by the Auditor himself. Each section should be carefully noted. Questions asked and answers given need to be recorded so that if queries arise in future, a clear answer can be given.

A well-kept set of audit working papers will normally have an index on the front setting out the contents in sequence. An example of such an index may be as follows:

XYZ CLUB

Accounts for the Year ended 31 December 1983

Schedule of Working Papers

1 Copy of Club Rules.
2 Copy of Memorandum and Articles of Association (if a Company limited by guarantee).
3 Copy of previous years accounts.
4 A schedule for each item, where relevant, in the final accounts, showing its make-up, existence, ownership, value or liability.
5 Copy of current accounts.
6 Bank reconciliation.
7 Extracts from minute book of important items.
8 Details of Club insurance policies in force.
9 Schedules of audit work performed.
10 Certificates given by Club or Treasurer re stocks, prepayments and accounts at Balance Sheet date.

Standing Back

When the Auditor has completed the detail work of the audit, it is essential to take time off to stand back and look at the 'whole'. This means that he should allow his mind to browse over all that he has done, checking first to see that nothing important has been omitted. Secondly, he should reflect on the information he has received. Has anything that he has been told or has discovered been inconsistent with other information? Small details, unimportant in themselves, sometimes come together to form a pattern or picture which might give a clue to other events. For example, the Cashier who never takes a holiday and who is most meticulous – Beware! Is he really such a virtuous person? It is just possible that he dare not be absent in case some ingenious fraud is discovered. Many frauds have been uncovered by management insisting that such a person takes a holiday. Subsequent enquiries may indicate that there is a probable connection. If the Cashier is known to like gambling, it is worth investigating.

The job of the Auditor is to spot weaknesses in the accounting system, and if the audit is done thoughtfully most of these should be reasonably apparent. The handling of cash requires special attention and a well-known area for fraud is in connection with the running of licenced bars where the methods of manipulation seem endless.

If weaknesses are discovered, or there are features of the accounting system that the Auditor feels should be brought to the attention of the committee, he should set these out in the form of a letter addressed to the committee, and subsequently discuss the matter with them. The Auditor has no power to compel the committee to make alterations, but if such points are sufficiently obvious, he may need to mention them in his audit report to the members, or at least give a qualified report.

The Audit Report

It has been assumed in this chapter that the club or association covered by these notes is not one subject to the Companies Acts 1948 to 1980 which require the Auditor to be professionally qualified.

The Honorary Auditor will need to consider the form of his audit report once the detail of the audit has been completed. The audit report is attached to the annual accounts and is normally the only means of formally communicating with the members, although the Auditor may well attend the annual general meeting and make his contribution if questions are raised on the accounts.

In the case of limited companies, the Auditor is required to undertake a detailed examination and review of the accounting records and draft final accounts with a view to forming an opinion on whether those accounts give a 'true and fair view' of the company's financial affairs during the period under review, and of the assets and liabilities on the Balance Sheet date.

If the Honorary Auditor feels that all is well, he should give a 'clean' report, meaning one without qualification. It should be expressed in clear, positive and simple language. One point to note is that it is not a certificate. He is not an insurer, guaranteeing the accuracy of the accounts.

An example of such a 'clean' report would be:

THE RACQUET TENNIS CLUB

Report to the Members

In my opinion the above accounts give a true and fair view of the state of the Club's affairs at 31 December, and of the excess of income over expenditure for the year ended on that date.

Hon. Auditor

There may well be an occasion when the accounts present a true and fair view with a specific exception. The Auditor may not be able to obtain all the information which he considers he needs. The report should clearly set out the information lacking and its effect upon the accounts, e.g.

'In the absence of the Treasurer, due to his illness, it has not been possible to verify the Cash in Hand. Subject thereto, in my opinion the above accounts give a true and fair view. . . .'

If circumstances are such that the accounts do not give a true and fair view, the report may well need to be worded to show the reason for this view, e.g.

'Due to the loss of certain files, it has not been possible to verify a large number of receipts and payments. In consequence, in my opinion the above accounts do not give a true or fair view of the state of the Club's affairs. . . .'

CHAPTER 10

Charitable Clubs and Taxation

During the last few years there has been an increase in the number of clubs and associations seeking to become charitable trusts or to operate a charitable trust in conjunction with the main body. The purpose has been to take advantage of the tax relief and other benefits available.

The object of the trust must fall within the legal definition of the term 'charitable'. Trusts which are charitable were classified in *Commissioners for Special Purposes of Income Tax* v *Pemsel* (1891) as:

1 Trusts for the advancement of religion
2 Trusts for the advancement of education
3 Trusts for the relief of poverty
4 Trusts for other purposes beneficial to the community not falling under any of the other heads (i.e. Conservation Societies and Archaeological Excavation Societies)

It should be realised that the rules relating to charitable trusts are strictly applied, especially as to the relationship of officials and members of the charitable society or trust to financial benefit arising from it. Consequently it is not always possible to bring the activities of a club or association within these heads.

To create a charitable society or trust it is necessary to draft a constitution or trust deed which will meet the requirements of the Charity Commission for registration under the Charities Act 1960. It is essential that such constitution ensures that if a society or trust is wound up its surplus assets are passed to another charity.

Under section 9, the Charity Commissioners may refer the draft deed to the Inland Revenue for their opinion in contentious cases.

A useful point to note is that under section 5(1) registration raises a conclusive presumption that an institution is a charity so long as it is on the register.

While clubs and associations may operate directly as charitable trusts, it is quite common to find that the trust merely provides the main source of income for an allied body. Frequently such a body is a limited company formed under the Companies Acts 1948 to 1980, being a company limited by guarantee and not having a share capital. This combination may give a more flexible organisation than one completely operated under the law covering charities, which is somewhat restrictive.

The reliefs available to a charitable trust are set out below.

Rate Relief

Charities are entitled as of right to 50 per cent relief on rates provided the hereditaments are occupied by the charities for charitable purposes. (See section 40, General Rate Act 1967, as amended.) Local authorities under the Act may also allow further relief on the payment of rates chargeable on an even wider range of properties occupied by charities and non-profit-making bodies – section 40(5).

Fiscal Relief

(1) Capital gains tax

By section 360(2) Income and Corporation Taxes Act 1970 a charity is exempt from capital gains tax in accordance with section 145 Capital Gains Tax Act 1979, if the proceeds are applied for charitable purposes, or until any property ceases to be subject to charitable trusts.

Where a donor gives property to a charity he is exempt from capital gains tax on any increase in value during his period of ownership. (Section 146, Capital Gains Tax Act 1979.)

(2) Development Land Tax Act 1976

The object of the Act is to tax the realisation of the development of land, but with effect from 26 March 1980 charities are completely exempt from liability on disposals of interests in land. However, if the charity ceases to be a charity the exempt liability becomes chargeable provided that it does not exceed the market value of all the property still owned by the charity (section 111 Finance Act 1980).

(3) Capital transfer tax

Capital transfer tax was introduced by the Finance Act 1975 to replace estate duty as a capital duty arising on a person's death. However, unlike estate duty, it also affects a gratuitous transfer of capital in life as well. Such gratuitous transfers are taxed cumulatively throughout a person's lifetime and on his death. These transfers are known as *transfers of value.*

Charities are entitled to a number of exemptions from capital transfer tax provided that a gift to a charity is outright or is given in trust exclusively for charitable purposes.

The main reliefs are:

1 Where a donor makes lifetime gifts to a charity more than one year before his death, they are wholly exempt from liability to the tax.
2 Gifts made to a charity within a year of the death of the donor or by his will, are exempt up to £200,000 as from 26 March 1980.
3 Charitable trusts are not subject to capital distributions or periodic charges (Finance Act 1975, Schedule 5, para. 20).

The effect of donating part of a person's estate to a charity is that the rate of any capital transfer tax payable on the rest of the estate will be reduced, which may encourage the making of gifts to charities.

A point worth remembering is that if a married couple wish to donate their estate to a charity after the death of the survivor, no capital transfer tax will be payable providing the surviving spouse's estate does not exceed £200,000.

(4) Income tax

A charity is specially exempt for income tax and corporation tax purposes by section 360, Income and Corporation Taxes Act 1970.

Rents on land vested in trustees for charitable purposes are exempt if applied to those purposes – section 360 1(a).

There is exemption from tax under Schedule B on land occupied by a charity – section 360 (1) (b).

Perhaps the most important exemptions are under section 360 (1)(c) on interest dividends and annuities and company distributions. Upon filing a repayment claim, tax deducted from source and tax credits on company dividends is repaid to the charity provided, of course, the charity applies the income only for charitable purposes.

Section 360 (1) (c)(ii) grants relief under Schedule D in respect of any yearly interest or other annual payment.

Where a charity carries on a trade, its profits under Schedule D will be exempt under section 360 (1)(e), providing:

(a) that the trade is exercised in the course of actually carrying out the primary purpose of the trust, or
(b) the work in connection with the trade is mainly carried on by the beneficiaries of the charity.

(5) Deeds of covenant

As was mentioned above, charities are largely exempt from income tax on their income, and this includes donations made by individuals and companies under deeds of covenant. A deed of covenant is a deed made by a donor whereby he covenants to pay the charity a sum of money each year, from which income tax is deducted, or deemed to be deducted. To be allowable as an annual charge, and thus a reduction of the donor's liability to income tax, the covenant had to be capable of 'exceeding six years' and not to be revocable. This long period has been a great handicap to charities as many people have not been prepared to commit themselves to a liability so far into the future. With high annual rates of inflation the only way the value of a covenanted gift could be raised has been to enter into an additional covenant which then ran for a further seven-year period.

This restraint on charitable giving has long been recognised, and as from 6 April 1980 the covenant period for tax purposes has been reduced from a period of 'over six years' to 'over three years'. (Section 55 Finance Act 1980.) Non-charitable covenants are not affected by the new rules. Unfortunately, it is still necessary to enter into an additional covenant; the opportunity was not taken to make it possible to alter the amount of an existing covenant.

However, it is possible to draft a deed for four years or some other period, whichever is shorter, relating to the donor's circumstances, but which are outside his control.

The reader needs to be aware that there are two methods of covenanting income. First, the gross is fixed, and from that figure tax is deducted at basic rate so that only the net is paid to the charity. At the same time, the donor completes a tax deduction certificate and gives this to the charity with the payment. In due course the charity sends the certificate to the Inspector of Taxes in support of a repayment claim.

An example of the 'gross' method is thus:

Gross amount covenanted	100
Less income tax @ 30%	30
Net	£ 70

A tax deduction certificate (Form R185(E)) for £30 will be completed by the donor and sent with his remittance to the charity.

The second method is to word a deed which provides that the net sum should always be the same. For example, a deed may provide that the gross shall be 'such an annual sum as after deduction of income tax will leave the net sum of £10'. If the basic rate of income tax is 30 per cent, the gross is calculated as $\frac{100}{70} \times £10$, which is £14.29. This can be shown as:

Gross	14.29
Less income tax @ 30%	4.29
Net	£10.00

A form R185(E) for £4.29 would thus be completed by the donor.

The majority of deeds of covenant follow the second method, which is simpler as donors do not have to recalculate the amount of their next contribution if there is a change in the rate of tax. In practice, many club treasurers will prepare a form R185(E) for the donor to sign, thus ensuring that the club gets a certificate of tax deducted for the correct amount. This method also facilitates payment by banker's order.

From 1981/82 income tax relief at rates above the basic rate will be allowable in respect of covenanted gifts to charities by individuals (section 56 Finance Act 1980). These reliefs will be subject to a maximum of £3000 per annum gross gifts. The purposes of this relief are to encourage individuals in the higher tax brackets to give to charities and to increase the yield of the gifts to the charities. An example will make this clearer, assuming the donor is liable to income tax at the 50 per cent rate of tax and that he makes a covenant at a net cost to himself of £300 per annum. Under previous legislation a 'net' covenanted gift of £300 per annum would give rise to a tax repayment to the charity of £128.57 at the basic rate of 30 per cent. This is calculated as $\frac{100}{70} \times £300 = £428.57$, and the process is called *grossing up*. The £428.57 represents the gross to the charity, so that the difference between the £300 paid and this figure is the tax deducted of £128.57. As a check on the calculation, tax on the £428.57 should be worked out at 30 per cent which, of course, comes to the £128.57

Under the new relief, if the donor wishes to make the gift more tax effective to the charity and at the same time keep the net cost to himself the same, he should increase his covenanted sum to £420. It works this way:

The donor is deemed to have made a gross gift of £600 so that, obtaining tax relief at 50 per cent, the net cost is still £300. So far as the charity is concerned, this deemed gross must have tax deducted at basic rate. Thus, if the basic rate is 30 per cent, tax to be deducted will be £180 (30 per cent × £600) and a form R185(E) is prepared, leaving the £420 to be covenanted. The total benefit to the charity will be £600.

The donor will receive his tax relief in the form of the £180 deducted at source, and a further tax relief of £120 to make up the £300 due to him. Where, however, the donor does not wish to increase his covenanted sum, the gross will remain at £428.57, but he will be entitled to tax relief at 50 per cent – £214.28. This will be made up by the £128.57 deducted at source and a further £85.71 (£214.28 – £128.57) relief. The charity will continue to receive a total of £428.57.

To assist charities in making repayment claims, the Inland Revenue introduced a simplified procedure in 1973. Under this, the form R185(AP) which is signed by the covenantor need only be submitted to the Revenue on the occasion of the first claim, provided the net sum is under a given figure. This is £130 for payments after 5 April 1979. The charities must, however, give an undertaking that proper accounting records are maintained which are available to the Revenue for inspection, if required.

a well-run committee can provide a great source of help and experience in the running of some specific task. On the other hand, if it contains some determined characters it is better to dispense with a committee as it will tend to be very time-consuming and inefficient.

This rather leads to the club having to make up its mind on the organisational structure which best suits its needs. Of course, if it is a limited company or trust, these needs will already largely be determined by company or charity law which will insist on a formal structure in organisation. However, this leaves many small clubs and organisations to consider.

Most clubs will require two types of meetings. There will be regular committee meetings, say once a month, in which there are only a few people involved. Then there will be general meetings of members, including the annual general meeting. In addition, from time to time, special topics or events will require specific information to be prepared and circulated in the club.

It is now possible to return to question 2 – 'What information should a report contain?' By looking at the needs of a committee and a general meeting of members in more detail, the principal contents common to most clubs will emerge.

It is assumed that most clubs will have one or more committees to conduct the running of the organisation. This may be a Management or General Committee which usually meets fairly frequently. The officers of the club are usually full members while the rest of the members of the committee are elected from the general body of club members. Information required by this type of committee will be used mainly for organisation and control. Thus, the Treasurer will be closely involved as much of the information will be financial.

Probably the most helpful information is a summary of the club's receipts and payments during the period, rather along the lines of the Bank summary in the Frendlee Club example, although that example is rather ambitious and covers a whole year. Figures for debtors or creditors should likewise be provided. If there are a series of Cash or Bank accounts, including Investment or Deposit accounts, these should be clearly stated in full and brought up to date, including interest received.

There is great merit in holding regular committee meetings at which the Treasurer is required to produce a factual report. He is obliged to keep the books up to date, with a definite reporting date, and the committee can see where the club is going financially, taking such action, if any, as it sees fit. Members, too, feel happier in their minds if they feel that the club finances are known by others, apart from the Treasurer. It reduces the chance of suspicion, which all too often raises its ugly head.

This type of report will, of necessity, need to include a reasonable amount of detail, mainly figures. Should the Treasurer provide any explanatory information? With small committees, it is common practice to circulate committee members with a report largely consisting of factual, figurative information, leaving explanations until the actual meeting, when the Treasurer gives his explanation verbally. This method has the advantage that it reduces the material to be circulated to basic essentials, and the

Treasurer can be questioned at the meeting. However, sometimes it will be necessary to commit explanations, comments or opinions to paper. The best guide and advice to the Treasurer responsible for such a report is to be brief and to the point.

Depending on the nature of the information contained in the report, it may be worth considering whether it should be made available to a wider audience by perhaps putting a copy on a notice-board for interested club members to read. Due to the perverse nature of the average person, after a while the reports will probably remain on the notice-board month by month unread by anyone. Then someone will get up one day and complain that members do not know what is going on, and we are back to question 1 – 'Why is a report needed?'

For the larger clubs, especially those operating a bar, the Bar Committee should require proper returns be prepared, at least once a month, giving trading results and stocks. Reference should be made to Chapter 7 on this subject as such reports are very important in the context of control and good management.

Reports for general meetings of members require less detail, as the average person finds large quantities of figures highly confusing. Even if he gets the information, very often he is not able to find it or appreciate its real significance. This has been found to be true in the case of the glossy annual reports and accounts produced by public companies. Some of these may run to thirty or forty pages of interesting information, but most shareholders will read the directors' report, the net profit for the year and the rate of dividend. Next step, the waste-paper basket. All the hard work and expense in the production of that information is wasted. The lesson, therefore, is keep it simple and highlight the main points.

An example of such a report is given below, one which would be useful for a fairly small club or society, such as 'The Get Weaving Society' mentioned in Chapter 5. Some clubs prefer to circulate a separate Treasurer's report, while others may wish to include the report with a general report to members, attaching the accounts as schedules.

THE GET WEAVING SOCIETY

Accounts for the Year ended 30 September Year 9

Treasurer's Report

Members will see from the attached Income and Expenditure account that the Society had an excess of expenditure over income for the year of £128. The primary reason for this figure is the deficit of £200 in the item for Courses & Speakers. As these courses have proved to be very popular and the speakers are national authorities in their fields, your Committee proposes to maintain the courses at the present level, but recommend that course fees should be raised to a more realistic figure.

To provide the Society with more adequate funds, your Committee further propose that subscriptions should be raised to £5 per year with effect from 1 October.

Hon. Treasurer

This type of report immediately brings to members' attention the main feature that the Society's finances are in a poor shape. By including the proposed remedies, much debate is saved with members making innumerable and often useless suggestions. Members, too, cannot complain that they were not warned when they are asked to pay higher charges and subscriptions in due course.

As a Judge said in a famous case at the turn of the century, give 'information, not means of information'. He meant that if you give information, do not give it in such a way that it merely makes the reader ask for more. Clarity and precision are the watchwords of good report writing.

Appendix — The Frendlee Club

A detailed example of the books and accounts of a typical club, from cash-book entries to the final accounts.

Diary of Events   THE FRENDLEE CLUB   *Schedule (A)*

Autumn and Spring Programme

Meetings held every Wednesday and Friday

October	4	Fancy Dress Party and Dance
	20	Visit to London – Sightseeing and Theatre Party
November	15	Whist Drive
	22	Choir Rehearsal for Xmas Carol Concert
	29	Coffee Morning – Sale of Work for Xmas Gifts to Old-Age Pensioners
December	6	Choir Rehearsal
	15	Theatre Party
	20	Dance and Party
	22	Carol Concert
	23	Christmas Lunch
	31	New Year's Party
January	10	Film Show – Holidays to Far-Away Places
	19	Demonstration of Spinning and Weaving
	24	Visit to Pantomime
	26	Dance
February	7	The Strolling Players – Two One-Act Plays
	14	Ladies' Darts Match
	23	Gentlemen's Cookery Competition
March	7	Festive Hat Making Demonstration
	14	Making Easter Cakes
	23	Easter Bonnet Competition
	30	Visit to Zoo
April	4	Whist Drive
	11	Dance and Social
	13	Film – Aspects of the Social Services
	27	Talk – Your Garden in Summer
May	9	Annual General Meeting and Social
	16	Dance
	25	Evening Walk – Buildings of Historical Interest in the City Centre
	31	End of Season Dance

Statement of Affairs as at 30 September Year 1

	Dr. £	Cr. £
Amplifier and equipment	850.00	
Billiard table and equipment	1400.00	
Table tennis equipment	120.00	
Darts board	15.00	
Electric kettle, crockery, cutlery and kitchen equipment	225.00	
Furniture	875.00	
Whist tables	200.00	
Records and tapes	460.00	
Members subscriptions in advance re Year 2		45.00
Treasurer's expenses re Year 1		19.00
Insurance prepayment – 1 month	11.00	
Cash at Bank – Deposit account	875.00	
do. – Current account	214.00	
Stock of food	28.00	
Accumulated Fund		5209.00
	£5273.00	£5273.00

Summary of Bank Account for the Year ended 30 September Year 2

	£	£	£		£
Balance brought forward				Rent	720.00
30 September Year 1			214.00	Rates	359.50
Subscriptions received		991.50		Heat & light	960.00
Sale of refreshments	235.41			Visits by members	1348.50
Sale of surplus food				Food & refreshments	
from dance	26.35	261.76		(general)	207.23
Billiard fees		113.50		Food & refreshments for	
Table tennis fees		44.85		dances & socials	509.33
Whist drive receipts		46.25		Purchase of records &	
Dances		716.50		tapes	148.05
Socials		832.29		Water rate	45.00
Donations received		500.00		Insurance	176.00
Coffee mornings		44.17		Xmas lunch	332.00
Receipts re visits by members		1348.50		Hire of bands	135.00
Members' Xmas lunch		332.00		Stationery	91.54
Carol concert		26.30	5257.62	Donation	15.00
				Repairs to billiard table	54.00
				Transfer to Deposit	
				account	150.00
				Treasurer's expenses	76.79
				Secretary's expenses	31.76
					5359.70
				Balance carried down	
				30 September Year 2	111.92
			£5471.62		£5471.62

Balance brought down 30 September Year 2		111.92

Schedule (D)

Summary of Bank Deposit Account for the Year ended 30 September Year 2

	£	£
Balance brought forward 30 September Year 1		875.00
Add Transfer from Current account during the year		150.00
		1025.00
Add Interest received		
31 December Year 1	45.00	
30 June Year 2	52.00	97.00
Balance carried forward 30 September Year 2		£1122.00

Schedule (E)

Schedule of Assets and Outstandings at 30 September Year 2

	£
Repairs to billiard table	37.30
Purchase of additional loud speaker	270.00
Stationery – Stationers Ltd	13.47
Stock of food	17.00

(a) Income and Expenditure Account for the Year ended 30 September Year 2

	£	£		£	£
Rent		720.00	Members' subscriptions		
Rates		359.50	(£991.50+£45.00)		1036.50
Heat & light		960.00	Sale of refreshments	235.41	
Water rate		45.00	*Less* cost		
Insurance (176+£11.00−			(£207.23		
$\frac{1}{12}$×£176.00=£14.60)		172.40	+28.00+17.00)	218.23	17.18
Stationery			Billiards receipts	113.50	
(£91.54+£13.47)		105.01	Table tennis		
Donation		15.00	receipts	44.85	158.35
Repairs to billiard table			Whist drive receipts		46.25
(£54.00+£37.30)		91.30	Xmas carol concert		26.30
Treasurer's expenses			Coffee mornings		44.17
(£76.79−£19.00)		57.79	Donation – Annie Smith		
Secretary's expenses		31.76	decd		500.00
			Proceeds of dances	716.50	
Depreciation			Proceeds of socials	832.29	
Amplifier & equipment	112.00			1548.79	
Records & tapes	121.61				
Games equipment	153.50		*Less* cost of		
Furniture & kitchen			refreshments		
equipment	130.00	517.11	(£509.33 − 26.35)		
				482.98	
			Hire of bands	135.00	617.98	930.81
			Receipts re members'		
			outside activities	1348.50	
			Less cost	1348.50	—
			Members' Xmas lunch		
			Receipts	332.00	
			Less cost	332.00	—
			Bank Deposit account		
			interest		97.00
					2856.56
			Excess of Expenditure over		
			Income for the year		218.31
		£3074.87			£3074.87

(b) Balance Sheet as at 30 September Year 2

Accumulated Fund	£		*Fixed Assets*	£	£
Balance at 30 September			Amplifier & equipment as at		
Year 1	5209.00		30 Sept. Year 1	850.00	
Less Excess of Expenditure over			Additions during year	270.00	
Income during the year	218.31			1120.00	
	4990.69		*Less* depreciation @ 10%	112.00	1008.00
Current Liabilities					
Sundry creditors			Records & tapes as at 30		
(£37.30 + £13.47)	50.77		Sept. Year 1	460.00	
Sound Ltd – loud speakers	270.00	320.77	Additions during year	148.05	
				608.05	
			Less depreciation @ 20%	121.61	486.44
			Games equipment as at 30		
			Sept. Year 1	1535.00	
			Less depreciation @ 10%	153.50	1381.50
			Furniture & kitchen equip-		
			ment as at 30 Sept.		
			Year 1	1300.00	
			Less depreciation @ 10%	130.00	1170.00
					4045.94
			Current Assets £		
			Bank – Current		
			account	111.92	
			– Deposit		
			account	1122.00	1233.92
			Stock of food	17.00	
			Prepayment	14.60	1265.52
	£5311.46				£5311.46

(*Schedule (F)* illustrates the traditional 'horizontal', or 'double entry', type of layout of an Income and Expenditure Account and Balance Sheet.)

(*Schedule (G)* is included to show the same information as in Schedule (F), but in modern vertical form.)

Schedule (G)

(a) Income and Expenditure Account for the Year ended 30 September Year 2

Income	£
Members' subscriptions	1037
Proceeds of dances & socials	931
(Note 1 overleaf)	
Donation – Annie Smith deceased	500
Bank Deposit account interest	97
Games receipts (Note 2 overleaf)	205
Xmas carol concert	26
Coffee mornings	44
Miscellaneous receipts	17
	2857

Less Expenditure	£	£	
Rent	720		
Rates	360		
Heat & light	960		
Insurance	173		
Water	45	2258	
Secretarial expenses & stationery		194	
Repairs to billiard table		91	
Donation		15	
Depreciation of fixed assets		517	3075
(Note 3 overleaf)			

Excess of Expenditure over Income for the year £218

(b) Balance Sheet as at 30 September Year 2

Fixed Assets (Note 5 overleaf)			£
Amplifier & equipment			1008
Records & tapes			486
Games equipment			1382
Furniture & kitchen equipment			1170
			4046

Add Current Assets		£	
Bank – Current account		112	
do. – Deposit account		1122	
Stock of food		17	
Prepayment		14	
		1265	

Less Current Liabilities	£		
Sundry creditors	50		
Sound Ltd – loud speakers	270	320	945
			£4991

Represented by:
Accumulated Fund

Balance at 30 September Year 1	5209
Less Excess of Expenditure over Income during the year	218
	£4991

(c) Notes

1 *Proceeds of Dances and Socials*	£	£	£
Proceeds of dances		717	
Proceeds of socials		832	
		1549	
Less Cost of refreshments	483		
Hire of band	135	618	
		£931	

2 *Games Receipts*			
Billiards		114	
Table tennis		45	
Whist drive		46	
		£205	

3 *Depreciation of Fixed Assets*			
Amplifier & equipment		112	
Records & tapes		122	
Games equipment		153	
Furniture & kitchen equipment		130	
		£517	

4 (a) Receipts re Members' outside activities		1349	
Less Cost		1349	
(b) Members' Xmas Lunch receipts		332	
Less Cost		332	

5 *Fixed Assets*

Amplifier & equipment as at 30 September Year 1		850	
Additions during year		270	
		1120	
Less depreciation for the year @ 10%		112	1008
Records & tapes as at 30 September Year 1		460	
Additions during year		148	
		608	
Less depreciation for the year @ 20%		122	486
Games equipment as at 30 September Year 1		1535	
Less depreciation for the year @ 10%		153	1382
Furniture & kitchen equipment as at 30 September Year 1		1300	
Less depreciation for the year @ 10%		130	1170
			£4046

Schedule (H)

Ledger Accounts Recording Transactions for Year 2

Accumulated Account

		£				£
Yr 2			Yr 1			
Sept. 30	I & E A/c excess of Expenditure over Income for the year	218.31	Sept. 30	Bal b/f		5209.00
	Balance c/d	4990.69				
		£5209.00				£5209.00
			Yr 2			
			Sept. 30	Bal b/d		4990.69

Rent

		£			£
Yr 2			Yr 2		
Sept. 30	Bank	720.00	Sept. 30	Tfr I & E A/c	720.00

Rates

		£			£
Yr 2			Yr 2		
Sept. 30	Bank	359.50	Sept. 30	Tfr I & E A/c	359.50

Members' Subscriptions

		£				£
Yr 2			Yr 1			
Sept. 30	Tfr I & E A/c	1036.50	Sept. 30	Bal b/f (subscriptions in advance re Yr 2)		45.00
			Yr 2			
			Sept. 30	Bank		991.50
		£1036.50				£1036.50

Heat and Light

		£			£
Yr 2			Yr 2		
Sept. 30	Bank	960.00	Sept. 30	Tfr I & E A/c	960.00

Water Rate

		£			£
Yr 2			Yr 2		
Sept. 30	Bank	45.00	Sept. 30	Tfr I & E A/c	45.00

Insurance

		£			£
Yr 1 Sept. 30	Balance b/f (Prepayment)	11.00	Yr 2 Sept. 30	Tfr I & E A/c	172.40
Yr 2 Sept. 30	Bank	176.000	Sept. 30	Prepayment ($\frac{1}{12}\times$ £176.00) c/d	14.60
		£187.000			£187.000
Yr 2 Sept. 30	Prepayment b/d	14.60			

Cost of Refreshments

		£			£
Yr 1 Sept. 30	Stock of food b/f	28.00	Yr 2 Sept. 30	Tfr I & E A/c	218.23
			Sept. 30	Stock of food c/d	17.00
Yr 2 Sept. 30	Bank	207.23			
		£235.23			£235.23
Yr 2 Sept. 30	Stock of food b/d	17.00			

Sale of Refreshments

		£			£
Yr 2 Sept. 30	Tfr I & E A/c	235.41	Yr 2 Sept. 30	Bank	235.41

Billiards Receipts

		£			£
Yr 2 Sept. 30	Tfr I & E A/c	113.50	Yr 2 Sept. 30	Bank	113.50

Table Tennis Receipts

		£			£
Yr 2 Sept. 30	Tfr I & E A/c	44.85	Yr 2 Sept. 30	Bank	44.85

Whist Drive Receipts

		£			£
Yr 2 Sept. 30	Tfr I & E A/c	46.25	Yr 2 Sept. 30	Bank	46.25

Stationery

		£			£
Yr 2			Yr 2		
Sept. 30	Bank	91.54	Sept. 30	Tfr I & E A/c	105.01
Sept. 30	Creditor c/d	13.47			
		£105.01			£105.01
			Yr 2		
			Sept. 30	Creditor b/d	13.47

Donations Paid Out

		£			£
Yr 2			Yr 2		
Sept. 30	Bank	15.00	Sept. 30	Tfr I & E A/c	15.00

Repairs to Billiard Table

		£			£
Yr 2			Yr 2		
Sept. 30	Bank	54.00	Sept. 30	Tfr I & E A/c	91.30
Sept 30	Creditor c/d	37.30			
		£91.30			£91.30
			Yr 2		
			Sept. 30	Creditor b/d	37.30

Treasurer's Expenses

		£			£
Yr 2			Yr 1		
Sept. 30	Bank	76.79	Sept. 30	Creditor b/f	19.00
			Yr 2		
			Sept. 30	Tfr I & E A/c	57.79
		£76.79			£76.79

Secretary's Expenses

		£			£
Yr 2			Yr 2		
Sept. 30	Bank	31.76	Sept. 30	Tfr I & E A/c	31.76

Sundry Receipts

		£			£
Yr 2			Yr 2		
Sept. 30	Tfr I & E A/c	70.47	Sept. 30	Bank (Xmas carol concert)	26.30
			Sept. 30	Coffee mornings	44.17
		£70.47			£70.47

Donations Received

		£			£
Yr 2			Yr 2		
Sept. 30	Tfr I & E A/c	500.00	Sept. 30	Bank – Annie Smith decd	500.00

Dances and Socials

		£			£
Yr 2			Yr 2		
Sept. 30	Bank – cost of refreshments	509.33	Sept. 30	Bank – Dances	716.50
			Sept. 30	do. – Socials	832.29
Sept. 30	Hire of bands	135.00	Sept. 30	do. – Sale of	
Sept. 30	Tfr I & E A/c	930.81		refreshments	26.35
		£1575.14			£1575.14

Members' Outside Activities

		£			£
Yr 2			Yr 2		
Sept. 30	Bank	1348.50	Sept. 30	Bank	1348.50

Members' Xmas Lunch

		£			£
Yr 2			Yr 2		
Sept. 30	Bank	332.00	Sept. 30	Bank	332.00

Bank Deposit Account

		£
Yr 1		
Sept. 30	Bal. b/f	875.00
Dec. 31	Interest	45.00
		920.00
Yr 2		
Feb. 16	Tfr C/A	100.00
		1020.00
June 30	Interest	52.00
		1072.00
Sept. 11	Tfr C/A	50.00
		1122.00

Bank Interest Received

		£				£
Yr 2			Yr 1			
Sept. 30	Tfr I & E A/c	97.00	Dec. 31	D/A		45.00
			Yr 2			
			June 30	D/A		52.00
		97.00				97.00

Amplifier and Equipment

		£				£
Yr 1			Yr 2			
Sept. 30	Balance b/f	850.00	Sept. 30	Tfr I & R A/c – Depre-		
Yr 2	Sound Ltd c/d			ciation @ 10%		112.00
Sept. 30	(creditor)	270.00	Sept. 30	Balance c/d		108.00
		£1120.00				£1120.00
Yr 2			Yr 2			
Sept. 30	Balance b/d	1008.00	Sept. 30	Sound Ltd b/d		
				(creditor)		270.00

Records and Tapes

		£				£
Yr 1			Yr 2			
Sept. 30	Balance b/f	460.00	Sept. 30	Tfr I & E A/c Deprecia-		
Yr 2				tion @ 20%		121.61
Sept. 30	Bank additions	148.05	Sept. 30	Balance c/d		486.44
		£608.05				£608.05
Yr 2						
Sept. 30	Balance b/d	486.44				

Games Equipment

		£				£
Yr 1			Yr 2			
Sept. 30	Balance b/f	1535.00	Sept. 30	Tfr I & E A/c Deprecia-		
				tion @ 10%		153.50
			Sept. 30	Balance c/d		1381.50
		£1535.00				£1535.00
Yr 2						
Sept. 30	Balance b/d	1381.50				

Furniture and Kitchen Equipment

		£				£
Yr 1			Yr 2			
Sept. 30	Balance b/f	1300.00	Sept. 30	Tfr I & E A/c Deprecia-		
				tion @ 10%		130.00
			Sept. 30	Balance c/d		1170.00
		£1300.00				£1300.00
Yr 2						
Sept. 30	Balance b/d	1170.00				

(a) Bank Receipts

Date	Detail	Bank	Subs.	Sale of Refresh-ments	Billiard Fees	Table Tennis	Whist Drive
		£	£	£	£	£	£
Yr 1							
Oct. 1 Balance b/f		214.00					
4 Dance tickets £1 each	166.00						
Receipt book nos 79–85	9.00		9.00				
Sale of surplus food	26.35			26.35			
6	3.69	205.04		2.14	1.25	0.30	
11	2.64			1.69	0.75	0.20	
13	5.79			3.19	2.05	0.55	
18 Receipt book nos 86–106	35.25		30.00	2.65	1.95	0.65	
		43.68					
20 Visit to London – travel & theatre £8 per head (122 members)		976.00					
20	3.80			2.95	0.75	0.10	
25	6.88			3.43	2.40	1.05	
27	4.59			1.79	2.05	0.75	
		15.27					
Nov. 1 Receipt book nos 107–129	40.14		34.50	2.44	2.10	1.10	
3	6.27			3.87	1.85	0.55	
8	9.05			4.35	3.15	1.55	
10	7.65			3.90	2.70	1.05	
		63.11					
15	41.70			13.60	0.50	0.10	27.50
17	7.02			3.47	2.75	0.00	
22	7.76			4.86	1.65	1.25	
24	6.25			3.25	2.25	0.75	
		62.73					
29	52.82			5.25	1.95	1.45	
Dec. 1	4.27			2.47	0.85	0.95	
		57.09					
6	8.44			3.74	2.95	1.75	
15 Theatre visit 57 @ £3	171.00						
15	6.76	186.20		4.26	1.65	0.85	
20 Xmas dance 218 @ £1	218.00						
20	2.69			2.14	0.55		
		220.69					
c/f		2043.81	73.50	101.79	36.10	15.75	27.50

the Year ended 30 September Year 2

Dances	Socials	Dona-tions	Coffee Mornings	Sun-dries	Visits	N.L.	Xmas Lunch	Proceeds of Carol Concert	Cash Contra
£	£	£	£	£	£	£	£	£	£
						214.00			
166.00									
					976.00				
			44.17						
					171.00				
218.00									
384.00			44.17		1147.00	214.00			

Date	Detail	Bank	Subs.	Sale of Refreshments	Billiard Fees	Table Tennis	Whist Drive
	£	£	£	£	£	£	£
b/f		2043.81	73.50	101.79	36.10	15.75	27.50
22 Carol concert	26.30						
23 Xmas lunch 83 @ £4	332.00						
		358.30					
31 New Year's party 197 @ £3		591.00					
Yr 2							
Jan. 3	9.42			4.87	3.05	1.50	
3 Receipt book nos 130–205	228.00		228.00				
5	7.04			3.89	2.60	0.55	
		244.46					
10 Film show	10.19						
10	6.47			4.07	1.80	0.60	
12	5.01			3.51	1.25	0.25	
		21.67					
12 Receipt book nos 206–286	243.00		243.00				
17 Demonstration of weaving	7.46						
17	8.75			6.10	2.15	0.50	
		259.21					
19	8.70			5.40	1.95	1.35	
24 Visit to pantomime 67 @ £2	134.00						
24	3.00			1.75	1.25		
26 Dance 135 @ £1	135.00						
26	5.90			2.75	2.40	0.75	
		286.60					
31 Receipt book nos 287–325	117.00		117.00				
Feb. 2	6.84			3.64	1.95	1.25	
7 2 plays 124 @ 75p	93.00						
7	7.47			4.17	2.35	0.95	
		224.31					
9	5.08			2.98	1.75	0.35	
9 Receipt book nos 326–378	159.00		159.00				
14	6.46			3.61	1.90	0.95	
14 Ladies darts match	17.45			6.35	2.25	0.25	
		187.99					
c/f		4217.35	820.50	154.88	62.75	25.00	27.50

Dances	Socials	Dona-tions	Coffee Mornings	Sun-dries	Visits	N.L.	Xmas Lunch	Proceeds of Carol Concert	Cash Contra
£ 384.00	£	£	£ 44.17	£	£ 1147.00	£ 214.00	£	£ 26.30	£
							332.00		
	591.00								
	10.19								
	7.46								
					134.00				
135.00									
	93.00								
	8.60								
519.00	710.25		44.17		1281.00	214.00	332.00	26.30	

Date	Detail		Bank	Subs.	Sale of Refreshments	Billiard Fees	Table Tennis	Whist Drive
		£	£	£	£	£	£	£
	b/f		4217.35	820.50	154.88	62.75	25.00	27.50
16		2.81			2.06	0.75		
21		7.58			4.23	1.95	1.40	
23	Gentlemen's cookery competition	12.25						
23		5.61			3.61	1.45	0.55	
28		5.89			3.74	1.90	0.25	
			34.14					
Mar. 2		7.65			4.40	2.35	0.90	
2	Receipt book nos 379–413	105.00		105.00				
7		6.13			3.63	2.05	0.45	
9		4.38			2.93	1.45		
			123.16					
14	Making Easter cakes	5.60						
14		6.38			3.23	1.90	1.25	
16		6.65			3.95	1.75	0.95	
			18.63					
21		7.92			4.47	2.20	1.25	
23		10.17			7.22	1.95	1.00	
23	Easter bonnet competition	17.60						
28		6.74			4.19	1.70	0.85	
30		2.74			2.09	0.65		
30	Visit to zoo 54 @ £1.25	67.50						
			112.67					
Apr. 4		5.34			3.14	1.70	0.50	
4	Whist drive	18.75						18.75
6		9.06			4.81	2.25	2.00	
11	Dance & social	68.43						
11		6.04			3.74	1.55	0.75	
			107.62					
13		7.03			4.03	2.75	0.25	
13	Film – 'Aspects of the Social Services'	14.05						
13	Annie Smith decd – legacy	500.00						
			521.08					
	c/f		5134.65	925.50	220.35	93.05	37.35	46.25

Dances	Socials	Donations	Coffee Mornings	Sundries	Visits	N.L.	Xmas Lunch	Proceeds of Carol Concert	Cash Contra
£	£	£	£	£	£	£	£	£	£
519.00	710.25		44.17		1281.00	214.00	332.00	26.30	
	12.25								
	5.60								
	17.60								
					67.50				
54.50		13.93							
	14.05								
		500.00							
573.50	773.68	500.00	44.17		1348.50	214.00	332.00	26.30	

Date	Detail	Bank	Subs.	Sale of Refreshments	Billiard Fees	Table Tennis	Whist Drive
		£	£	£	£	£	£
b/f		5134.65	925.50	220.35	93.05	37.35	46.25
18		4.68		2.43	1.80	0.45	
20		8.11		5.06	2.50	0.55	
27	Talk – 'Your Garden in Summer'	5.70					
		18.49					
27		6.40		4.05	1.70	0.65	
29		4.41		2.76	1.45	0.20	
May 2		4.86		3.16	1.25	0.45	
4		5.93		3.78	1.40	0.75	
		21.60					
9	A.G.M. & Social	49.16					
9		3.37		2.07	1.10	0.20	
11		7.71		4.01	2.40	1.30	
16	Dance 114 @ 50p	57.00					
16		5.26		3.06	1.45	0.75	
		122.50					
18	Receipt book nos 414–435 New members	66.00	66.00				
23		7.84		4.59	2.05	1.20	
		73.84					
25		5.49		3.54	1.70	0.25	
25	Evening walk – Buildings of historical interest	3.75					
31	End of season dance 86 @ £1	86.00					
31		5.30	100.54		2.90	1.65	0.75
		5471.62	991.50	261.76	113.50	44.85	46.25

Yr 2
Sept. 30 Balance brought down   111.92

Dances	Socials	Dona-tions	Coffee Mornings	Sun-dries	Visits	N.L.	Xmas Lunch	Proceeds of Carol Concert	Cash Contra
£	£	£	£	£	£	£	£	£	£
573.50	773.68	500.00	44.17		1348.50	214.00	332.00	26.30	
	5.70								
	49.16								
57.00									
	3.75								
86.00									
716.50	832.29	500.00	44.17		1348.50	214.00	332.00	26.30	

111.92

(b) Bank Payments

Date		Total	Rent	Rates	Heat & Light	Visits	Food & Refreshments (General)
		£	£	£	£	£	£
Yr 1							
Oct. 1	S.T.O. re City Council	60.00	60.00				
5	Water Co. – half-year's water rates to 31 Mar.	22.50					
7	Dance Committee – food for beginning of season	72.14					
9	Supermarket Ltd – coffee, tea, biscuits, etc.	10.99					10.99
10	S.T.O. re S.W.E.B. – storage heating & lighting	80.00			80.00		
15	Dairy Ltd – milk	2.23					2.23
17	Corner Shop Ltd	1.75					1.75
18	City Council – half-year's rates to 31 Mar.	162.50		162.50			
19	Motor Coaches Ltd – hire re visit to London theatre	84.00				84.00	
	Playboy Theatre Ltd 122 tickets	892.00				892.00	
25	Records Ltd – 5 × L.P.s	25.75					
Nov. 1	S.T.O. re City Council	60.00	60.00				
4	Supermarkets Ltd	4.17					4.17
7	Corner Shop Ltd	3.08					3.08
10	S.T.O. re S.W.E.B.	80.00			80.00		
12	Dairy Ltd	5.16					5.16
22	Safeguard Insurance Co. Ltd – Insurance year to 31 Oct. Yr 2	176.00					
30	Corner Shop Ltd	7.44					7.44
Dec. 1	S.T.O. re City Council	60.00	60.00				
3	Dairy Ltd	4.53					4.53
10	S.T.O. re S.W.E.B.	80.00			80.00		
13	Laughter Theatre Ltd	171.00				171.00	
14	Fillem Caterers Ltd re Xmas lunch	332.00					
18	Dance Committee – food for Xmas dance	94.74					
	c/f	2491.98	180.00	162.50	240.00	1147.00	39.35

Food re Dances & Socials	Records	Repairs	Water	Insur- ance	Xmas Lunch	Hire of Band	N.L.	Station- ery	Dona- tions	Cash Contra
£	£	£	£	£	£	£	£	£	£	£
			22.50							
72.14										
	25.75									
				176.00						
					332.00					
94.74										
166.88	25.75		22.50	176.00	332.00					

Date	Total	Rent	Rates	Heat & Light	Visits	Food & Refreshments (General)
	£	£	£	£	£	£
b/f	2491.98	180.00	162.50	240.00	1147.00	39.35
23 Bob's Jolly Country Band re dance	60.00					
23 Supermarkets Ltd	8.49					8.49
Yr 2						
Jan. 1 Social Committee – Food re New Year's Eve party	256.85					
1 S.T.O. re City Council	60.00	60.00				
6 Swing U Band re New Year's party	75.00					
10 S.T.O. re S.W.E.B.	80.00			80.00		
14 Billiard Supplies Ltd – repairs to billiard table	54.00					
15 Dairy Ltd	6.73					6.73
15 Supermarkets Ltd	8.75					8.75
18 City Records 6 × L.P.s	32.70					
21 Town Theatre 67 tickets re pantomime	134.00				134.00	
22 Corner Shop Ltd	3.81					3.81
29 Printers Ltd – stationery	64.00					
Feb. 1 S.T.O. re City Council	60.00	60.00				
4 Corner Shop Ltd	1.24					1.24
6 Amateur Players – donation towards expense of 2 plays	15.00					
10 S.T.O. re S.W.E.B.	80.00			80.00		
12 Dairy Ltd	4.19					4.19
15 Supermarkets Ltd	22.09					22.09
16 Transfer Deposit A/c	100.00					
25 Corner Shop Ltd	14.53					14.53
Mar. 1 S.T.O. re City Council	60.00	60.00				
5 Dairy Ltd	9.75					9.75
10 S.T.O. re S.W.E.B.	80.00			80.00		
16 Corner Shop Ltd	7.44					7.44
28 Zoological Gardens 54 tickets to zoo	67.50				67.50	
Apr. 1 S.T.O. re City Council	60.00	60.00				
5 Water Co – half-year's water to 30 Sept.	22.50					
9 City Council – half-year's rates to 30 Sept.	197.00		197.00			
c/f	4137.55	420.00	359.50	480.00	1348.50	126.37

Food re Dances & Socials	Records	Repairs	Water	Insurance	Xmas Lunch	Hire of Band	N.L.	Stationery	Donations	Cash Contra
£	£	£	£	£	£	£	£	£	£	£
166.88	25.75		22.50	176.00	332.00					
						60.00				
256.85										
						75.00				
							54.00			
	32.70									
								64.00		
									15.00	
							100.00			
			22.50							
423.73	58.45		45.00	176.00	332.00	135.00	154.00	64.00	15,00	

Date	Total	Rent	Rates	Heat & Light	Visits	Food & Refreshments (General)
	£	£	£	£	£	£
b/f	4137.55	420.00	359.50	480.00	1348.50	126.37
10 S.T.O. re S.W.E.B.	80.00			80.00		
11 Supermarket Ltd	8.64					8.64
16 Dairy Ltd	4.77					4.77
19 Corner Shop Ltd	13.12					13.12
19 Dance Committee re food for dance & social	23.46					
20 City Records	89.60					
29 Treasurer's expenses	49.75					
30 Printers Ltd	27.54					
May 1 S.T.O. re City Council	60.00	60.00				
4 Supermarkets Ltd	22.47					22.47
7 Dairy Ltd	9.63					9.63
10 S.T.O. re S.W.E.B.	80.00			80.00		
16 Corner Shop Ltd	15.49					15.49
16 Dance Committee re food for dance	24.77					
22 Supermarkets Ltd	6.74					6.74
29 Dance Committee re food for dance	37.37					
June 1 S.T.O. re City Council	60.00	60.00				
10 S.T.O. re S.W.E.B.	80.00			80.00		
22 Secretary's expenses	31.76					
July 1 S.T.O. re City Council	60.00	60.00				
10 S.T.O. re S.W.E.B.	80.00			80.00		
27 Treasurer's expenses	27.04					
Aug. 1 S.T.O. re City Council	60.00	60.00				
10 S.T.O. re S.W.E.B.	80.00			80.00		
Sept. 1 S.T.O. re City Council	60.00	60.00				
10 S.T.O. re S.W.E.B.	80.00			80.00		
15 Transfer Deposit A/c	50.00					
	5359.70	720.00	359.50	960.00	1348.50	207.23
30 Balance carried down	111.92					

Food re Dances & Socials	Records	Repairs	Water	Insurance	Xmas Lunch	Hire of Band	N.L.	Stationery	Donations	Cash Contra
£	£	£	£	£	£	£	£	£	£	£
423.73	58.45		45.00	176.00	332.00	135.00	154.00	64.00	15.00	
23.46	89.60						49.75	27.54		
24.77										
37.37							31.76			
							27.04			
							50.00			
509.33	148.05	—	45.00	176.00	332.00	135.00	312.55	91.54	15.00	

Working Schedule re Preparation of Final Accounts from Incomplete Records

	Statement of Affairs		Bank Summary		Adjustments		Income & Expenditure Account		Balance Sheet	
	Dr.	Cr.	Dr.	Cr.	Dr.	Cr.	Dr.	Cr.	Dr.	Cr.
	£	£	£	£	£	£	£	£	£	£
Amplifier & equipment	850.00				270.00				1120.00	270.00
Depreciation on amplifier equipment							112.00			112.00
Records & tapes	460.00				148.05				608.05	
Depreciation on records & tapes							121.61			121.61
Games equipment	1400.00 / 120.00 / 15.00								1535.00	
Depreciation on games equipment							153.50			153.50
Furniture & kitchen equipment	225.00 / 875.00 / 200.00								1300.00	
Depreciation on furniture & kitchen equipment							130.00			130.00
Bank – Current A/c	214.00				5257.62	5359.70			111.92	
do. – Deposit A/c	875.00		150.00		97.00			97.00	1122.00	
Stock of food	28.00					28.00				
Insurance	11.00		176.00			14.60	172.40		14.60	
Treasurer's expenses		19.00	76.79				57.79			
Accumulated Fund		5209.00								5209.00
Members' subscriptions		45.00		991.50				1036.50		
Sale of refreshments				235.41				235.41		
Sales of surplus food from dance				26.35				26.35		

Item	£	£	£	£	£	£
Billiard fees	113.50					113.50
Table tennis fees	44.85					44.85
Whist drive receipts	46.25					46.25
Dances	716.50					716.50
Socials	832.29					832.29
Donation received – Annie Smith decd	500.00					500.00
Coffee mornings	44.17					44.17
Receipts & visits by members	1348.50		1348.50			1348.50
Members' Xmas lunch	332.00		332.00			332.00
Carol concert	26.30					26.30
Rent	720.00		720.00			
Rates	359.50		359.50			
Heat & light	960.00		960.00			
Food & refreshments (general)	207.23	28.00	218.23	17.00	17.00	
Food & refreshments re dances	509.33	148.05	509.33	148.05		
Records & tapes	148.05		45.00			
Water rate	45.00		135.00			
Hire of band	135.00	13.47	105.01			13.47
Stationery	91.54		15.00			
Donation (paid)	15.00		91.30			
Repairs to billiard table	54.00	37.30	31.76			37.30
Secretary's expenses	31.76					
	£5273.00	£5273.00	5617.93		5828.57	6046.88
		£5359.70	5399.62		*218.31	
		£5257.62	*218.31		218.31	
			£5617.93		£6046.88	£6046.88

* Excess of expenditure over income.

125

Index